Writers of Italy Series

General Editor
C. P. Brand
Professor of Italian
University of
Edinburgh

3
SVEVO

© B. Moloney 1974
Edinburgh University Press
22 George Square, Edinburgh

ISBN 0 85224 248 4

Printed in Great Britain by
R & R Clark Ltd.
Edinburgh

for J.M.M., I.J.M., and K.A.M.

Edinburgh University Press

Italo
SVEVO

A critical introduction

BRIAN MOLONEY

*

853.8
Sv 28
M738

DE 18 '90

Contents

	Preface	vii
1.	Essays and Explorations, 1861–90	1
2.	Plays, 1880–1926	16
3.	First Narrative Fiction, 1888–92	27
4.	*Senilità*, 1898	39
5.	The Years of Silence, 1898–1923	56
6.	*La coscienza di Zeno*, 1923	67
7.	Last Narrative Fiction, 1923–28	89
8.	Autobiography and Art	98
9.	Language, Style and Techniques	108
10.	Italo-German Novelist : a Perspective	125
	Notes	131
	Select Bibliography	133
	Index	137

PUBLISHER'S ACKNOWLEDGMENTS

Thanks are due to Dall'Oglio Editore for permission to quote from the *Opera omnia* edition of Svevo's works, and to Martin Secker and Warburg Ltd. for permission to quote from the *Standard Edition* and from P. N. Furbank's *Italo Svevo. The Man and the Writer*; to the Hogarth Press Ltd. and Basic Books, Inc., for permission to quote from *The Complete Psychological Works of Freud*; to David McKay, Inc., for permission to quote from H. B. and A. C. English, *A Comprehensive Dictionary of Psychological and Psychoanalytical Terms: A Guide to Usage*; to Penguin Books Ltd. for permission to quote from L. N. Tolstoy's *Anna Karenin*; to University of Chicago Press for permission to quote from W. C. Booth, *The Rhetoric of Fiction* and R. R. Wisse, *The Schlemiel as Modern Hero*.

Preface

Angus Wilson recently drew up a list of what he regarded as the fifty most important twentieth-century novels. In a select first division of works which he thought worthy to stand beside those of the great masters of the nineteenth century, he found room for only one novel by an Italian. It was *La coscienza di Zeno* by Italo Svevo.

There have so far been two attempts to introduce the English-speaking public to the novels of Svevo. The years 1929–32 saw the appearance in English of a few of his short stories and of two novels, *La coscienza di Zeno* (*Confessions of Zeno*, translated by Beryl De Zoete, London 1930), and *Senilità* (*As a Man Grows Older*, translated by Beryl De Zoete, London 1932). There followed a series of respectful, even at times warm, reviews by V. Sackville-West, Arnold Bennett, Frank Swinnerton, L. P. Hartley, L. A. G. Strong, and Winifred Holtby, and others. After 1933 there was almost total silence on the English literary scene as far as Svevo was concerned. He attracted slightly more attention in the United States, but in general terms it can safely be said that in both countries it was only what Stendhal might have called 'the happy few' who read Svevo.

The same was true of Italy too, and what happened in England and America was a natural reflection of what was happening in Svevo's own country. But in the post-war period Svevo gradually came into his own, and he has now been accorded the status of a modern classic. A Uniform Edition of his works has been published in England, and 1966 saw the appearance of the first monograph on him in English – which is arguably the best biography of him in any language. Two novels, at the time of writing, have become available in paperback editions.

Yet still he is not widely read. The translations of his works sell in a steady trickle, no more. Now I do not believe that he will ever be a 'popular' novelist in the manner of, say, Moravia, or other Italian novelists who have become well known here. Svevo is more demanding than they; but he is, conversely, more satisfying, and I find it strange that English novel-readers, whose tastes are often adventurous, should read Camus and Sartre, or Mann and Musil, but not

Svevo, just as they seldom or never read Verga, that other great novelist neglected by the English. The purpose of this book is to provide the English reader with a critical account of Svevo's works which both takes account of recent criticism and scholarship and also offers a personal view. I hope it will go some way towards explaining why it is that he bears no obvious resemblance to any other Italian novelist and will suggest the perspectives within which he may most profitably be considered.

My grateful thanks are due to Svevo's daughter, Signora L. Svevo Fonda Savio, for access to her father's manuscripts, for her willingness to answer my queries and for permission to reproduce an illustration of her father as frontispiece to this volume. I also wish to thank the General Editor of the Writers of Italy series, Professor C. P. Brand, who has encouraged and advised me, and Mr J. A. Gatt-Rutter of the department of Italian in the University of Hull, who read my typescript and made valuable comments and suggestions. I am indebted to so many friends and colleagues in the Faculty of Arts in the University of Leeds that it is invidious to mention names: nevertheless, mention must be made of Mr S. Lowy of the Department of Semitic Studies, Professor J. R. Wilkie and his colleagues in the Department of German, and Mr A. Fryer of the Department of Italian.

My thanks are also due to the staffs of the Brotherton Library of the University of Leeds, particularly of the Inter-Library Loan Section, and of the Biblioteca Civica Attilio Hortis of Trieste for their unfailing assistance. Much of my work in Trieste was made possible by grants from the research fund of the Department of Italian in the University of Leeds.

I also have pleasure in acknowledging my debt to my wife, who has read this book at every stage from typescript to proof, and to Mrs Brenda James and Mrs L. Decunha who typed the manuscript. Nor would I omit to mention my Triestine friends, whose hospitality has made my visits to that city so memorable.

B.M. *Leeds March, 1973*

NOTE. All quotations from Svevo's works, unless otherwise indicated, are taken from the *Opera omnia* published by Dall'Oglio, Milan (see Bibliography, p. 133 for details). References in the text are to volume and page numbers.

1. Essays and Explorations, 1861–90

Italo Svevo is the pseudonym – or, more precisely, one of the pseudonyms – of the Triestine Jewish novelist Aron *detto* Ettore Schmitz. Almost everything in that statement needs comment or explanation. Why describe him as Triestine, rather than Italian? Why did he use a pen-name, and do his real and assumed names tell us anything important about him? Why stress his Jewishness? The answers to these questions are all linked, and will go some way towards explaining Svevo's choice of subject-matter and of literary techniques.

Svevo was born in Trieste in 1861 and became an Italian citizen only in 1918, when Austria surrendered Trieste to Italy. The city, which had previously been part of the Austro-Hungarian Empire, had been proclaimed an Imperial Free Port in 1719, but its prosperity dated from 1749, when Maria Theresa granted it special privileges and tax exemptions. Thereafter it rapidly increased in size and importance and nineteenth-century prints and photographs of the city show busy quays and a sky-line bristling with masts, although its decline, which began about 1850, accelerated catastrophically after unification with Italy left it a port without a hinterland. The size, wealth and influence of the Jewish community in Trieste provide a useful index of the city's prosperity. Its rapid growth, and the relatively greater freedom enjoyed by Jews in the Austrian Empire, attracted to Trieste a large colony of Jewish merchants, who formed the largest of the city's minority groups. The progressive emancipation of the Jews throughout Europe led still more to settle there. Most Triestine Jews were, or soon became, Italian-speaking, and tended to support irredentist movements; Theodor Mayer, for example, who in 1881 founded the newspaper *Il Piccolo*, was a Hungarian Jew. In Trieste, as elsewhere in Europe, they made a contribution to the cultural life of the city in which they lived which was totally out of proportion to their numerical importance. Yet their situation was not without its disadvantages. Long and bitter memories of centuries of persecution had created a distrust of the Gentile which was matched only by a desire to be submerged in the mainstream of European culture. When the Jews emerged from the ghetto they encountered European culture at one of its periodic high points – but at a moment when positivism in science and philosophy seemed bent on undermining traditional religious beliefs, whether Christian or Jewish. Mixed marriages, conversions to Christianity or loss of faith in traditional beliefs made Jewish communities less clearly defined and there ensued a collective crisis of assimilation and identity not unlike that reflected in the work of such American Jewish novelists as Henry and Phillip Roth and Norman Mailer. And with the decline in the prosperity of Trieste in the second half of the last century, the sense of social insecurity acquired a financial as well as a psychological dimension.

All this is to some extent exemplified in the life of Svevo. His paternal grandfather, Adolfo Schmitz, probably came from the Rhineland. In Treviso he married a Rosa Macerata, whose name shows that she too was Jewish. Adolfo's son Francesco, according to Svevo, thought of himself as Italian and married an Italian-speaking Jewish girl. Svevo's parents were both practising Jews and Francesco occupied a prominent place in the local Jewish community. His four surviving daughters married into Jewish families and his sons almost certainly went through the ceremony of *bar-mitzvah* to mark their religious coming of age at thirteen. In 1880 Francesco Schmitz went bankrupt and Ettore was obliged to take an uncongenial post in the Trieste branch of the Unionbank of Vienna. He had by this time lost whatever religious faith he had once had. Lack of faith and the absence of a sense of the numinous is something with which we in our society are all too familiar, but for a first-generation unbeliever in that most believing and most persecuted of communities the experience must have been disturbing. Chaim Barmant, writing of the Schmitz family's co-religionists in nineteenth-century England, has said that as their religion became less vital, the children 'suffered the small discomfitures of being a Jew, without any of the consolations of Judaism'.[1] One of the discomfitures, in Svevo's case, consisted of belonging to an unbelieving minority within a believing minority group. Ironically enough he was nevertheless on one occasion refused a job on the grounds that he was a Jew. The wry tone in which Svevo in his correspondence alludes to his racial origins suggests that he found his Jewishness something of a burden. That he jokes about it does not invalidate the observation; Svevo is rarely more serious than when he jests, and his humour is often a defence mechanism.

In some ways Svevo's position was made easier in 1896, when he married his second cousin Livia Veneziani. Yet in other ways the marriage made his position more difficult. It is a measure of Livia's love that although she was a devout Catholic she accepted a civil wedding with her fiercely anti-clerical fiancé – a devotion which was rewarded when Svevo, simply to please his wife, and not out of conviction, allowed himself to be baptized. But Livia's parents were wealthy, and Svevo belonged to the poorer branch of the family and found it difficult to support his wife. If the relatively privileged Siegfried Sassoon, always aware of the presence of numerous wealthy Sassoon relatives, could complain of his 'sense of inferiority', how much more justified was Svevo's alarm at the 'inferiorità sociale' which his marriage was to bring him (III, *784*).

Yet when writing about himself and his pseudonym in the *Profilo autobiografico* of 1928, Svevo never mentions his Jewishness. He hints at it in his misleading description of his father as 'assimilated'. Writing of himself in the third person (the *Profilo* was originally drafted by his journalist friend Giulio Cesari and then rewritten by himself), the novelist wrote: 'Al suo pseudonimo "Italo Svevo" fu indotto non dal suo lontano antenato tedesco, ma dal suo prolungato soggiorno in Germania nell' adolescenza' [His pseudonym 'Italo Svevo' was prompted not by his remote German ancestor but by his prolonged stay in Germany during his adolescence]. The name means 'Italus the Swabian' or 'The Italo-German', and in the *Profilo* Svevo explains that his father had sent him to a college near Würzburg. In Trieste he had attended Jewish schools until 1873. Francesco Schmitz had no doubts as to what his sons were to do in life; like him, they were to go into business in Trieste. And since they had so far been brought up to speak chiefly Triestine dialect and Italian, and since fluent German was essential for their careers, he decided to send them away to continue their education. He admired German culture and education, and so his choice fell not on an Austrian establishment, which for a Triestine would not have been unusual, but on the Brüsselische Handels- und Erziehungsinstitut at Segnitz-am-Main, which at that time catered mainly, but not exclusively, for Jewish students. In 1873 three of the Schmitz brothers – Ettore, Adolfo and Elio – were sent there. Elio stayed only for a few months, but Ettore remained for five years. At Segnitz he became fluent in German and read widely in German literature as well as in other literatures in German translation. In this way he was able to read authors as diverse as Shakespeare and Gogol, and it was in German, too, that he was able to read much science, sociology and philosophy. It was either in Germany, or shortly after his return to Trieste, that Schopenhauer became one of his favourite authors; Svevo tells us that it is perhaps to the German philosopher that we owe the pseudonym Italo Svevo, which appeared for the first time on the novel *Una vita* (1892).

Svevo was devoted to his mother, and Jonard has suggested that separation from her at the age of eleven, at the behest of his father, had a profound psychological effect upon the impressionable boy, turning him against society in general and inducing in him an inferiority complex and a sense of guilt which was at once provoked by and at the same time justified, the feeling that he had been abandoned. This is partly conjecture, based on a perhaps over-facile identification of Svevo with the characters of his novels. The most direct literary echo of the separation is to be found in the autobiographical story *L'avvenire dei ricordi* (1925), which does indeed hint at the discovery of an inferiority on his part, in the sense that Roberto, aged eleven and a half, who in the story stands for Svevo, is to be looked after by Armando, aged thirteen, who stands for his brother Adolfo, whereas he had expected some independence. Svevo referred to his neurotic tendencies metaphorically in his letters and diaries as his 'rane'. They consisted of a sense of dissatisfaction, a conviction of his own inferiority and weakness, a tendency to hypochondria (which made him worry about his health for the rest of his life and read as much as he could about the latest developments in medicine), an addiction to smoking – or perhaps one should say an addiction to giving up smoking – a feeling that he was prematurely old, and a longing for a love based on understanding and tenderness. Psychological health and illness achieved in Svevo a delicate balance: his neurotic tendencies were strong enough to make him wish to write in order – amongst other things – to externalize and so to understand or transcend his problems; but they were never so strong as totally to inhibit his creative powers or to make what he wrote merely the expression of neurotic weakness.

These tendencies may well have been exacerbated by separation from his mother, but they were not the only consequences of his stay in Germany. When he returned to Trieste in 1878 he had read widely in European literature and was full of ambitions for a literary career which almost at once met with what at the time seemed to be a setback. Having been brought up to speak Triestine at home – a Veneto dialect which then had a larger admixture of Croat than it does now – and then educated in Germany, he wanted urgently to visit Florence in order to improve his literary Italian, to 'rinse his clothes in the Arno' as Manzoni had done, and as several representatives of his and of the next generation of Triestine writers did, including Scipio

Slataper, Giani Stuparich, the painter-poet Virgilio Giotti, the poets Umberto Saba and Biagio Marin, Alberto Spaini, and Carlo Michelstaedter of Gorizia. But Francesco Schmitz's declining prosperity and the need for Ettore to earn his living denied him the luxury of a visit to Florence. In the long term this disappointment may have ensured his originality and independence as a writer, but in the short term it must have seemed a disaster and Svevo was left with something of a linguistic inferiority complex and an awareness that his knowledge of Italian language and literature was woefully inadequate.

Further study at the Istituto Revoltella in Trieste, ostensibly additional preparation for a business career, convinced Svevo that he was not cut out for the world of commerce, but it also provided time, which he badly needed, for studying the Italian classics. His reading was haphazard until he discovered the works of Francesco De Sanctis (1817–83), who was probably the most influential Italian critic of his day, and whose ideas and synthetical, as opposed to analytical, methods, are echoed and imitated by Svevo in the articles which he wrote for the Triestine newspaper *L'Indipendente* between 1880 and 1890. It was not so much that Svevo wished to familiarize himself with Italian literary traditions in order to imitate them as that he wanted both to improve his command of the language and to see how he could insert himself into those traditions. And his early essays show that he found himself in something of a dilemma.

By 1880 Svevo was enjoying the cultural life which Trieste had to offer. But what did Trieste have to offer? Little or nothing, thought Umberto Saba (1883–1957), who commented that 'La situazione di un triestino che scriveva per l'Italia da Trieste ... era difficile', since 'dal punto di vista della cultura, nascere a Trieste nel 1883 era come nascere altrove nel 1850', complaining that in his youth 'la città di Saba era ancora, per quel poco che aveva di vita culturale, ai tempi del Risorgimento : una città romantica', and that he lived in 'un ambiente dove nessuno aveva parlato a lui di buoni o cattivi autori'.[2] ['The position of a Triestine writing for Italy from Trieste was difficult' 'from the cultural point of view, being born in Trieste in 1883 was like being born elsewhere in 1850' 'Saba's city was still, as far as its limited cultural life was concerned, in the days of the Risorgimento : a romantic city' 'circles in which no one had spoken to him about authors good or bad'.] Can this be the same city as that described by Svevo in the *Profilo autobiografico*?

Trieste era allora un terreno singolarmente adatto a tutte le coltivazioni spirituali. Posta al crocevia di più popoli, l'ambiente letterario triestino era permeato dalle colture più varie. Alla 'Minerva' (la Società letteraria triestina) non si trattavano soltanto argomenti letterari paesani o nazionali. Le persone colte di Trieste leggevano autori francesi, russi, tedeschi, scandinavi ed inglesi. E nel piccolo ambiente si coltivava assiduamente e musica e pittura. Italo Svevo si trovò naturalmente attratto da tutti i cenacoli artistici e letterari della sua giovinezza. (III, *801*) [Trieste was in those days a soil singularly well suited to the cultivation of things of the mind. Situated at the cross-roads of several nations, Triestine literary circles were permeated by the most varied cultures. At the 'Minerva' (the Triestine literary society) not only local but national literary topics were discussed. Cultured people in Trieste read French, Russian, German, Scandinavian and English authors. Music and painting were diligently pursued in the small society. Italo Svevo was naturally attracted by all the artistic and literary coteries of his youth.]

This is not merely a case of the distance of old age lending enchantment to a youth which was not in reality as happy as it might have been; Saba was also viewing his youth from a similar distance. It is a matter of perspective. Saba considered culture to be Italian culture and thought of Trieste solely in relation to Italy, as though it were a cultural suburb of Florence. Naturally he found it provincial, in the pejorative sense, and from his point of view he was right. Trieste did lag behind Italy; its poets went on writing in the manner of Carducci long after the younger generation of Italian poets had shaken off the old master's yoke. Svevo, on the other hand, as a result of his background and education, is more cosmopolitan, and he is undoubtedly right to see Trieste as more European than Italian, and by virtue of that fact, paradoxically less provincial.

At all events, Svevo, a music-lover and an amateur violinist, frequented the 'circolo musicale', the concert-hall and the opera-house, as well as attending the 'circolo artistico', where he met painters and sculptors. As an aspiring man of letters he went to the 'Società di Minerva', which had been founded in 1810, where he heard lectures and discussions on a wide range of authors and topics. The texts of lectures given at the 'Minerva' were sometimes printed in *L'Indipendente*, the leading contributors to which were nearly all members, and it was natural that when Svevo had something ready for publication he should offer it to the newspaper. For *L'Indipendente*, which had been founded in 1877, was more than a newspaper; it was the expression of the essential *Italianità* of Trieste's Italian-speaking population, and to publish in it was an act of identification with Italy which had both political and cultural overtones.

That Svevo had something ready to publish was in itself remarkable. He had begun, or planned to begin, many poems, stories and plays, but in 1880 he had nothing but abandoned projects to show for his pains. What then so fired him in 1880 that he succeeded in getting into print? His first work was an essay entitled 'Shylock' and it appeared in *L'Indipendente* on 2 December.[3]

He was an enthusiastic theatre-goer in a city which supported at least three theatres. He had returned from Germany a passionate admirer of Shakespeare, and in that December he was looking forward to a performance of *The Merchant of Venice*. He must have been dismayed to hear it rumoured that it was not a suitable play to put on in Trieste since it might offend the Jewish element in the audience. Finally it was decided that the play would go on, and the confident tone of Svevo's essay derives partly from the fact that he belonged to the winning party, and partly from a desire to show how superior he was to bigotry and prejudice. The subject of the essay is the possibility of anti-semitism in Shakespeare's play, and Svevo, basing his treatment of it on Heine's essay on Jessica in *Shakespeares Mädchen und Frauen* (1838), argues that the dramatist was not consciously anti-semitic and that Shylock is essentially a tragic figure – as he has recently been interpreted by Laurence Olivier.

Between 1880 and 1890 Svevo wrote twenty-seven articles for *L'Indipendente*, as well as the essay 'Del sentimento in arte', written in 1887 but not published until 1954. Ettore Schmitz did not sign any of them with his own name. From 1880 until 1885 he signed himself 'E.S.'; from late 1886 he used the pseudonym 'E. Samigli', which he also used for the short stories *Una lotta* (1888) and *L'assassinio di Via Belpoggio* (1890), which were published in the same paper. It was as though Svevo wished to keep separate his two careers as bank employee and as man of letters, as though there were something professionally unbecoming in authorship. It is likely that he took to using his pseudonym in 1886 because of the possibility that his contributions might be confused with that of a certain Elio Staleno, who also wrote for *L'Indipendente*. Whether that accounts for the change or not, Svevo's first pen-name had a number of advantages. It retained his initials, thus concealing his identity from the general public but helping to reveal it to initiates; it concealed his Jewishness, which he felt as a burden; and it sounded suitably Italian for an Italian-language newspaper of irredentist sympathies, compelling the reader to accept Svevo for what he wanted to be – an Italian writer, not a Jew of Austrian or German descent.

Twenty-eight essays in a little over a decade might seem a meagre harvest, especially when one realizes that all but three were written in the period from 1883 to 1889. Yet his achievement is more impressive than might at first appear. He was not quite nineteen when he first began to publish, and if some of his ideas seem derived, what should surprise us is that they were derived from such a wide range of sources and presented in so confident a manner. Svevo, moreover, unlike the usual Italian man of letters, had no formal literary training and had little time for writing, especially after 1880. In addition, he spent some time almost every day until 1902 at the offices of *Il Piccolo*, going through foreign newspapers and compiling foreign news reports. And at the same time as he was working on these essays he was also busy with plays, short stories and, in the later years of the decade, his first novel.

These essays are our main source of information concerning Svevo's culture and development up to the time when he first began to publish fiction. Fame came late to Svevo, and so there is little information to be gleaned from the memoirs or diaries of his contemporaries: no-one at that stage thought him worth taking note of. His brother Elio's diary, of which only brief extracts have so far been published, contains some information, but not as much as we should like. His *Epistolario* includes only one letter written before 1895, and his wife's *Vita di mio marito*, written after his death, sheds little light on his youth. If we wish to know something of the cultural influences which shaped the budding novelist, of the dilemmas which he faced, we must have recourse to the essays.

Yet how representative are they? Svevo was not a professional reviewer, dealing with books as they came out, and one assumes that he felt free to avoid subjects he had no interest in. This explains some otherwise puzzling silences. He read such Italian magazines and periodicals as *Corriere della sera, Domenica del Fracassa, La Domenica letteraria* and *Nuova antologia*, so that he must have been aware of much that was being written in Italy. If, then, he chooses not to write about such authors as De Amicis and Fogazzaro, it must be not only that he finds them uncongenial – in fact he sometimes discusses writers he dislikes – but that they do not offer him the possibility of exploring topics which interest him.

The subjects which engage him most frequently are literary, but he ranges widely and one is struck by the variety of both subject and tone. Most of the essays have a serious air of intellectual commitment, offering balanced judgements with a maturity surprising in one so young. He is also capable of writing in polemical tone: in 'La verità' (1884) he takes issue with Renan; in ' "Il libro di Don Chisciotte" di E. Scarfoglio' (1884) he challenges his contemporary on the interpretation of Zola; in 'Critica negativa' (1888) he tilts at professional theatre critics. 'Giordano Bruno giudicato da Arturo Schopenhauer' (1885) is militantly anti-clerical. The incisive tone of these essays and their avoidance of normative methods suggest that Svevo had in mind as his models not only De Sanctis in Italy but also, possibly, French impressionist critics such as Anatole France and Jules Lemaître. At the other end of the tone-scale are the humorous pieces. 'Il signor Nella e Napoleone' (1887) is an affectionately ironical portrait of an old admirer of Bonaparte, and the last two essays are 'Sogni di Natale' (1889), which is a Christmas entertainment, and 'Echi mondani' (1890), in which Svevo, temporarily replacing the regular contributors to that column, writes in jesting fashion about one of his private preoccupations – addiction to smoking – with a light-hearted excursus on the influence of the cigarette on modern French literature.

Svevo's subjects are to some extent those which one would expect. That he should be interested in music is natural – had not Schopenhauer ranked music above the other arts? – but in his admiration for Wagner he is ahead of his time. There are references to the visual arts from the Renaissance to modern times. His interest in history, and especially in the cult of Napoleon, emerges in 'Per un critico' (1887), in which he is able to compare Taine, Thiers and Michelet on the subject. It will already be clear that he has an interest in philosophy – but philosophy in the widest sense, including positivist thought, Darwin and evolutionary theories, Herbert Spencer, Marx and social and political thought. And alongside these there is an interest in Schopenhauer (and possibly in Nietzsche, although this does not emerge from the essays) which demonstrates an awareness of the importance of the irrational and the subjective in the interpretation of history as well as in the arts. Six essays – 'Shylock' (1880), 'Riduzioni drammatiche' (1882), 'Il pubblico' (1883), 'Una commedia in lingua impossibile' (1884), 'Una frase sulla Mandragola' (1887) and 'Critica negativa' (1888) – deal with the theatre. Another eight – 'La "Joie de vivre" di Emilio Zola' (1884), ' "Il libro di Don Chisciotte" di E. Scarfoglio' (1884), 'Giorgio Ohnet' (1885), 'Un individualista' (1886), 'Le memorie dei fratelli Goncourt' (1887), 'La vocazione del conte Ghislain' (1887), 'L'Immortel' (1888), 'Mastro-don Gesualdo' (1889) – deal with novelists and novels, while two – 'Il dilettantismo' (1884) and 'Del sentimento in arte' (1887) – discuss general topics embracing both drama and the novel.

The emergence of a nucleus of recurrent themes gives the impression that Svevo's aim is only in part to inform the reader; in part he is attempting to resolve, or at least to define, some of the dilemmas which confront him as an aspiring author. Thus he poses the problem of reconciling success on the commercial level with artistic integrity. 'Il pubblico' and 'Il dilettantismo' are both of interest in this respect. The latter is a witty defence of the amateur writer. A certain sophistry enables him to classify Goethe, Machiavelli, Michelangelo and Alberti as amateurs, and his description of dilettantism is an interesting prelude to themes to come. There is also an amusing satirical sketch of the amateur keeping up with his reading – the recent Zola novel, many essays and the latest book by Carducci. But more important than that is the admission that the amateur secretly longs for fame, which he knows can come overnight. On that score many disappointments were in store for Svevo.

At two points in this essay it is difficult not to see a direct reference to his situation at the Unionbank. The bantering tone does not conceal his seriousness as he talks of Hamlet being acted by amateurs 'coadiuvati da qualcuno che sfoga degl'istinti che rimangono insoddisfatti scrivendo lettere di Banca e via di seguito' (III, 592) [assisted by someone who is giving expression to instincts which are not satisfied by writing letters for a bank and so on.] And later, after listing his 'amateurs', he asks (rhetorically): 'se tali uomini ... provarono il bisogno di coltivare altre materie, non è scusabile se un nostro agente di commercio o di banca soddisfa in quanto può quel desiderio di ridare idee e forme estetiche che madre natura, irragionevolmente, gli mise nel sangue?' (III, 594) [if such men ... felt the need to cultivate other subjects, is it not pardonable that some business or bank clerk should satisfy, as far as he can, that desire to express aesthetic ideas and forms which mother Nature unreasonably put into his blood?] Svevo, in other words, seeks in art a satisfaction he fails to find in his profession. He is also lured by the prospect of fame.

It would, however, be misleading to suggest that the quest for celebrity was Svevo's chief motive for writing, for in 'Giorgio Ohnet' he observes that to use art merely to gratify ambition is to treat it, in Schiller's phrase, as a 'butter-providing cow'. The artist's concern, in Svevo's view, must be with truth. It is on the grounds that Renan merely recognized, but did not love, truth that he attacks the French historian in 'La verità'. This essay was prompted by the report that Renan had expressed the wish that the epitaph 'Veritatem dilexi' be engraved on his tombstone, on the grounds that the love of truth had been the driving-force in his activities. This Svevo denies; he has read Renan's *Averroès* (1852), and takes obvious pleasure in accusing Renan, who believed anti-religious propaganda to be a crime, of adopting an Averroistic attitude of 'two truths' to his own work, thus rendering inefficacious all that he had accomplished. Contrast this attack on Renan, the idol of the positivists, with the tribute to Taine in 'Per un critico' : 'La sua dea è la verità e si può pensare ch'egli erri, non che'egli sia di mala fede' (III, *608*). [His goddess is truth, and one might think him mistaken, but not in bad faith.]

Truth, then, is for Svevo a consideration which over-rides all others, and the question of truth in art was one on which he thought long. He avoids, as Saccone has pointed out, the simplistic formula of art as a mirror held up to life. Nor does he equate the artist with the scientist, in the naturalist manner; like De Sanctis, he carefully distinguishes between them, and in defending Zola against the charge that he had set out in his novels to 'prove' Darwin's theories, replied that this was not so. 'Non scienziato ma artista, Zola descrive la vita servendosi di una teoria scientifica che gliela spiega. Se questa teoria venisse scartata da altra, i nostri posteri vedrebbero, nell'opera di Zola, una rappresentazione della vita quale la sentoni i più colti dei nostri contemporanei' (III, *590*). [An artist, not a scientist, Zola describes life making use of a scientific theory which explains it to him. If that theory were to be superseded by another, our descendants would see in Zola's work a depiction of life as it is seen by the most cultured of our contemporaries.] Svevo's argument is based on Zola's practice, not his theories – *sentono* implies a degree of subjectivity of which Zola the theorist might not have approved – and his admiration for the French novelist is not based on the cult of Naturalism. Zola, for Svevo, is a novelist whose work is rooted in the intellectual life of his time, who finds in the science of his day a conceptual framework in terms of which he can most effectively express his vision of life and thus remain faithful to his inspiration.

Svevo returns to this last point in the widely ranging 'Del sentimento in arte'. Inveighing against historical criticism and source-hunting, he points out that it is all too easy to state that Dante, Boccaccio and Shakespeare derived ideas and plots from earlier sources, but borrowings of this kind do not diminish the artist's originality. 'L'originalità risiede nel temperamento. Produca francamente; sarà originale o meno; artifiziosamente non lo diverrà mai' (III, 672). [Originality lies in the temperament. Let (the artist) write freely; he may be original or not; he will never become so by design.] Here Svevo comes close to formulating not simply the proposition that originality is compatible with the concept of working within a tradition but that the repudiation of one's literary heritage and the desire to express oneself only in one's own terms will militate against the creation of anything that could be called art. Subjectivity alone is not enough. This is probably why, in these essays, Svevo seems to be looking for literary models, for a tradition to which he can relate his work, and it is at this point that one sees most clearly the dilemmas to which I referred earlier. For within the Italian tradition, to which he most wished to belong, he found no models he could regard as appropriate to his own case.

As a theatre-goer and an intending dramatist, he could see that the surest way to achieve popular success was to write well-made plays in the manner of Victorien Sardou (1831–1908); but he found Sardou trivial and superficial. Annetta's excitement, in *Una vita*, at the prospect of seeing the first night of *Odette* (1881) in Paris is intended to reveal the superficiality of her culture. Sardou's success raises the question of the relationship between the dramatist and his audience – which Svevo feels to be more immediate than that between the novelist and his readers – and of the influence of the latter on the former. In 'Il pubblico' he argues that in general the public's taste is bad and that 'il contatto continuo in cui vengono specialmente da noi portati autori e spettatori non può essere che fatale all'arte' (III, 569), [the continual contact into which authors and spectators are continually brought, especially in our theatres, is bound to be fatal to art] since the author will tend to give the naturally conservative public what he thinks it wants. Italian dramatists, in Svevo's view, labour under another disadvantage. In 'Critica negativa' he states that the Italian dramatic tradition is weak: with Achille Torelli (1841–1922), Paolo Ferrari (1822–89) and Giuseppe Giacosa (1847–1906), it experienced something of a revival, but such signs of life as it showed were stifled by a school of criticism which was purely destructive. 'Il nostro teatro, per quanto inferiore, bisognava lasciarlo stare, vegetare come poteva ... Vale meglio qualche cosa, per quanto piccola, che nulla. Dal nulla nulla può svilupparsi.' [Our theatre, however inferior, should have been left alone, to vegetate as best it could ... Something, however small, is better than nothing.

Nothing can come of nothing.] The Shakespearian echo in that last sentence reveals Svevo's despondency.

In 'Riduzioni drammatiche' Svevo considers the plans of the *veristi* to solve the problem of the short supply of good plays by adapting for the theatre successful novels. He disapproves, on the grounds that the two forms, novel and play, are so different that any adapter needs not so much to put the novel into dialogue form as totally to recast it – and few adapters, especially the novelists themselves, are capable of doing this. He thus anticipates the verdict of modern critics on what Verga and Capuana were about to do, beginning with the former's *Cavalleria rusticana* in 1884. He was no prophet, however; his judgement was based on his knowledge of what had happened in the French theatre. The stage version of *L'Assommoir* in 1879 was the first of a series of plays from naturalist novels and how right Svevo was is shown by the fact that most were unsatisfactory.

Much of what has been said about Svevo and the theatre applies also to his exploration of the novel tradition. The now forgotten Georges Ohnet (1848–1918) seems to have been to the novel, in Svevo's eyes, what Sardou was to the theatre. In 1885, the year in which Ohnet published *La Grande Marnière* and *Le Maître de forges* (1882) reached its two hundred and fiftieth reprint, Svevo devoted to him a long essay in *L'Indipendente*. (Jules Lemaître launched his celebrated attack on Ohnet in the same year, some six weeks after Svevo.) Svevo seems to be asking two related questions. Why is Ohnet so popular? And does he write such bad novels, knowing that he has hit upon a successful formula, solely in order to gratify his ambition? Svevo attributes Ohnet's success to his ability to reassure his middle-class readers by presenting to them a picture of the world as they would like to think it is, secure and comforting, in which right, associated with bourgeois wealth and the established order of things, triumphs over wrong. 'È molto tranquillizzante!' [It's very tranquillizing!] is his sardonic comment. He answers the second question in the negative: Ohnet is so naïve as to believe in the idealized world of his own fiction.

Once again Svevo finds in a commercially successful writer a superficiality and a falsification of reality which are incompatible with his austere ideal of the high seriousness of art. And once again he is unable to find an Italian model to whom he can relate. De Amicis and Fogazzaro are not mentioned in the essays, but in the tale *Una burla riuscita* the hero reads their works to his invalid brother in order to send him to sleep; if Ohnet had been, metaphorically, a tranquillizer, they are sedatives in the literal sense. The modern reader naturally thinks of Svevo's two great Italian predecessors, Manzoni and Verga. In later years Svevo was inclined to attribute his youthful dislike of Manzoni, which he regretted, to the influence of Carducci. Verga he admired, as is shown by his review of *Mastro-don Gesualdo* in 1889, but he found the world of Verga's peasants too remote from his own. This is why he preferred *Mastro-don Gesualdo* to *I Malavoglia*: 'Ci troviamo in un contorno di nobili e popolani molto vicini alla borghesia; è un ambiente che ci è più vicino, più facile di quello del basso popolo di una provincia lontana'. [We find ourselves in aristocratic and working-class settings very near the middle class: it is a background which is near to us, more accessible than that of the proletariat of a distant province.] Svevo's decision to set *L'assassinio di Via Belpoggio* among the 'basso popolo' of Trieste may be a gesture in Verga's direction.

Svevo discusses the mature Verga in terms of Flaubert, Zola and impersonality. Nothing could be more natural than that Svevo should make his own one of the basic tenets of the novelists he most admired. Yet he also insisted, as we have seen, that originality lay in the artist's temperament, and went on: 'L'originalità non può quindi essere altro che la franca espansione di un carattere non affettato, non tolto a prestito. Si tratta di sincerità prima di tutto' (III, 672). [Originality cannot be anything other than the frank expression of an unaffected character, not a borrowed one. It is primarily a question of honesty.] Zola's attempts to construct an aesthetic based on the notion of impersonality have justly been described by F. J. W. Hemmings as infantile. If his dictum that 'Une œuvre d'art est un coin de la nature vue à travers un tempérament' [A work of art is a corner of nature seen through a temperament] had left the door ajar for subjectivity to enter, Svevo kicked it open. But there is a difference in the attitudes of the two writers. Zola, in his theoretical writings, could not reconcile the concepts of impersonality and subjectivity, and tended to neglect the latter, which in his practice was more important than he realized; Svevo, on the other hand, stresses both notions, and that he does not see them as incompatible is the result not of his naïveté but of his culture and his temperament, both of which led him to express himself in terms of irony. The novelists whom he most admired and imitated were Stendhal and Flaubert, both distinguished for their irony. His *Diario per la fidanzata* shows how quickly he perceived that irony was a source of strength: 'In quanto è spirito o forza, la mia parola non è altro che ironia' (III, 772–3). [In so far as it is wit or strength, what I have to say is nothing but irony.]

Svevo never attempted to work out the theoretical basis of an irony which could, if not reconcile opposites, at least set up between them a fruitful tension. He was impatient with theory, and in 1890 he ceased to write essays for *L'Indipendente*. His preliminary explorations were over and he was by now committed to drama and narrative fiction.

2. Plays, 1880–1926

Trieste in the last decades of the nineteenth century, with at least three theatres regularly staging plays, was one of the most important centres of Italian theatrical life. Play reviews in the city's newspapers are eloquent testimony to a well-developed interest in the theatre, and Triestine audiences were reputed to be demanding and discriminating. Plays figure prominently in Svevo's early reading, and he even at one time thought of taking up acting as a career. He seems to have been associated with amateur dramatic society performances in the 1880s, and his first essays were on theatrical subjects. His enthusiasm for the theatre was such that he talked of it as 'la forma delle forme ... la sola dove la vita possa trasmettersi per vie dirette e precise'.[1] [The form of forms ... the only one through which life can be communicated by direct and exact means.] What more natural than that he should attempt to write for it? His earliest known piece of writing, which dates from 1880, and so antedates all his narrative fiction, consists of the opening lines of a verse play, *Ariosto governatore*, and he left other plays unfinished at his death in 1928.

Svevo wrote thirteen plays, but he was not a successful playwright. Only one of his plays was performed during his lifetime. This was *Terzetto spezzato*, a one-act comedy which had a short run in Rome in April 1927. Svevo was unable to see any of the performances, which had only a lukewarm reception. The only play to be published during his lifetime was the monologue *Prima del ballo*, which was printed in *Befana 1891*, the New Year supplement to *L'Indipendente*. I assume, since it is so brief, that it was probably written especially for that supplement and it is appropriately light-hearted in tone. Four plays were published in periodicals in the 1930s – *Un marito* in *Il convegno* (Milan) in 1931, *Inferiorità* in *Le panarie* (Udine) in 1932, *Il ladro in casa* in *La porta orientale* (Trieste) in 1932, and *L'avventura di Maria* in *Il convegno* in 1937. They were not performed at the time and they were presumably read only by a small section of the Italian public, which in any case showed little interest at that time in Svevo. The awakening of interest in him after the Second World War led to the publication of two more plays, *Terzetto spezzato* and *Atto unico* in

1953 and 1954 respectively, again in periodicals – *Giovedí* (Rome) and *Ausonia* (Siena) – with a limited circulation. Six plays – *Le ire di Giuliano, Le teorie del conte Alberto, Una commedia inedita, La verità, Con la penna d'oro* and *La rigenerazione* – had to wait until the appearance in 1960 of the first collected edition of Svevo's plays. By this time he was recognized as a major author, and the interest stimulated by this volume led to a number of plays being performed. They did not have great success, and it is ironical that Svevo should owe such reputation in the theatre as he has mainly to Tullio Kezich's adaptation in 1965 of *La coscienza di Zeno*. The verdict of most critics has been that with the possible exceptions of *Inferiorità* and *Un marito* Svevo's plays are deficient in dramatic qualities and are of interest only in so far as they anticipate or echo the themes of his novels. Is this attitude justified? And if so, how is it that Svevo, whose novels are full of inner tension and dramatic conflict, failed so signally in the theatre?

There are, unfortunately, two serious obstacles in the way of a serious study of Svevo's plays. A play can hardly be judged solely as words on the printed page and without experience in the theatre – an experience which few are likely to have. Most readers will have to rely on the printed text. But the 1960 edition, reprinted as the fourth volume of the *Opera omnia* edition, is deficient in two respects. It fails to reproduce accurately the texts of Svevo's manuscript and typescript versions, omitting lines and exchanges of dialogue, and often 'improving' Svevo's Italian, and the dates to which the editor, A. Apollonio, assigns the plays are rather arbitrary. In the pages which follow I propose to survey the plays one by one, tentatively putting them into chronological order.[2]

On 10 February 1880 Svevo began work on *Ariosto governatore*, which was to be a play in verse set in the period the poet spent as governor of the Garfagnana from 1522 to 1525.[3] Since it was financial hardship which forced Ariosto against his wishes to take the post, the play may well have been intended to deal with the status of the artist in society. The choice of an Italian literary figure as hero is not surprising; Svevo at this time was reading much Renaissance literature and the popular Paolo Ferrari had written several plays of this kind on eighteenth-century subjects. Svevo may well have been influenced in his choice of subject by Goethe's *Torquato Tasso*. His decision to write in verse – and in the ponderous fourteen-syllable *verso martelliano* used by Ferrari and Giacosa – has occasioned some surprise, not only on account of his lack of skill in handling it, but also because of his reported aversion to poetry in general. This was never as strong in reality as it is reputed to have been; in his youth he wrote poems which have not survived, enjoyed Carducci and read Goethe's *Römische Elegien* with his fiancée. On 28 February, however, Svevo abandoned his projected play on Ariosto, having written only seventy lines of the first scene. His play depicts Ariosto in later life, but adds to the poet's disillusionment an anachronistic sense of social justice, which derives directly from Svevo's socialism, and a compassionate mind which refuses to avoid suffering by juggling with ideas.

Then followed a series of projected plays of which only the titles remain. The earliest completed ones to survive are a group of four which can be assigned to the same period but for which it is difficult to establish any precise order. The manuscript versions of three – *Le teorie del conte Alberto, Una commedia inedita* and *Le ire di Giuliano* – have survived in Trieste. The first two are written in a careful, round, schoolboyish hand on the same type of paper. The style of all three is full of archaisms, but the hand of *Le ire di Giuliano* seems more mature (or more careless). All three must belong to the same period, with *Le ire* being written, or copied out, last. Apollonio assigns the latter to 1881 on the basis of a date which he claims to have seen on the manuscript and which in fact does not exist.[4] These plays are signed 'E. Samigli', which suggests that in their present form they date from the period 1886–92 in which Svevo is known to have used that pseudonym.

Le teorie del conte Alberto is a light *scherzo drammatico* in two acts. Alberto, Count of Wolfenbüttel, was brought to Italy for health reasons at the age of twelve. He has settled there, dedicated himself to the study of science, and believes implicitly in the notion of heredity. In Trieste he has fallen in love with Anna, the daughter of Elivira Tremagli and ward of his friend Lorenzo Migliori. Lorenzo, who knows of his faith in Darwinism, first tells him – untruthfully – that Anna's father was a fraudulent bankrupt who committed suicide in prison after gambling his money away. Finding that Alberto still wishes to marry the girl, his honesty compels him to reveal the truth, namely that Anna's mother had had several lovers and that he is himself Anna's father. Like mother, like daughter? Alberto decides that love and Anna's self-evident goodness are to guide his conduct, not an abstract scientific law.

One should not expect too much from a *scherzo*, but even so this one has little to commend it. One could perhaps link its attack on statistics with Svevo's fable (1897) of the old man who loses all his capital through no fault of his own and who is reduced to suicide only when Herbert Spencer, the philosopher and economist, who was still alive in 1897, explains to him that the 'social law' demands the suppression of the weak and that no compassion or help can be extended to him. The fable catches Spencer's pretensions to omniscience very well and, like the play, is a protest against the over-rigid application of supposedly scientific, but inhumane, doctrines to human beings. On the other hand, the characters in *Le teorie* are not well developed and have an air of caricature about them. Svevo's dialogue lacks sureness and the proliferation of exclamation marks is very revealing, as though the tyro hopes that his style may be made more effective by them. The padding in the middle scenes makes one believe that the play would have been more effective in one act.

Una commedia inedita is another *scherzo drammatico*, this time in one act. It is based on a trite situation – that in which a husband arrives home unexpectedly and catches his wife with another man. On this unoriginal theme Svevo weaves his original variations. Elena Penini is no ordinary wife; she refuses to be treated by either husband or admirer as a mere chattel, and resents the former's failure to consult her on matters of importance. Her admirer, Adolfo, is an aspiring dramatist of the 'verist' school. He wants uncritical admiration from her, and is disconcerted when she gives him good advice and an honest, and unfavourable, assessment of his play, from which Svevo's comedy takes its title. Penini at last realizes his wife's worth and will in future treat her as an equal. This, perhaps because of its greater conciseness, is the only one of these early plays to have been performed; in September 1967 it was put on in Rome, with *La verità* and *Inferiorità*, in an evening of Svevo one-act plays.

Le ire di Giuliano is another domestic comedy, with Lucia leaving her husband on account of his violent temper. This distresses the other members of her family, who are financially dependent on Giuliano, but a sudden reconciliation puts an end to their distress and to this insubstantial play. Svevo's attack on what he seems to have regarded as the current style of marriage is that it is a materialistic arrangement which leaves no more room for emotion than a contract between businessmen. Svevo was perhaps led to deal with problems of this kind by the influence first of Paolo Ferrari, who after his historical plays went on to deal with social problems, and then of Ibsen, several of whose plays were performed in Trieste in the 1890s. Equally, the examples of Pietro Cossa and Sem Benelli may have suggested that, for him at least, there was no future as a historical dramatist.

Il ladro in casa, the last of the early plays, is more substantial.

Subtitled *Scene della vita borghese*, its four short acts depict the activities of the swindler Ignazio Lionelli. Lionelli is an opportunist, not a rebel; he despises bourgeois commercial morality but has no alternative values to offer except those of an unscrupulous egoism. Partly because of this, and partly because his victims are so passive and gullible, the play lacks tension. The subtitle implies a fragmentary structure, as well as a satirical intention which is partly realized, in that the motives of almost all the characters, whether marrying, giving in marriage or eloping, are mercenary. This is true even of the values which Lionelli's wife asserts in the last act, as she repudiates her husband : 'Mi sento libera di agire secondo la mia coscienza e secondo giustizia. Non più dissimulazioni, non più misfatti! Non lasciarlo fuggire, Carlo! Egli ha con se trentamila franchi e sono tuoi!' (IV *123*). [I feel free to act according to my conscience and justice. No more dissembling, no more misdeeds! Don't let him get away, Carlo. He's got thirty thousand francs on him and they are yours!] Lionelli is a worthless character, but his function is to expose the moral bankruptcy of those he exploits.

Prima del ballo, which was written to be read, rather than for the stage, needs little comment, other than the reflection that the early plays may well have been written with publication in *L'Indipendente* in mind. But with *L'avventura di Maria* we have a more complex, more typically Svevian play than any we have discussed so far. A three-act play dating from the period 1891–1901, *L'avventura* was first performed in 1966. The Maria of the title is a young concert violinist who visits an old school-friend, Giulia, now married to a businessman, only to discover that Giulia's husband, Alberto Galli, is the man who had made advances to her while he was away from home on business. The affair becomes more serious; Maria loses her customary composure and her two concerts in the provincial town are a failure. She invites Alberto to flee to South America with her, but he, who is accurately described by his wife as 'a good bourgeois who is attached to his regular life', refuses; casual infidelity is one thing, serious commitment another. The ironical twist to the plot is Maria's motivation; she longs – temporarily – for a middle-class home life. Love was to be her means of escape into routine. Svevo has some difficulty in bringing about his dénouement, however; after convincingly showing Giulia as the offended wife who will lose her husband rather than sacrifice her notions of dignity, he makes her extend to Alberto a forgiveness which comes too quickly to be convincing.

Terzetto spezzato was written between 1892 and 1925.[5] Its theme is, once more, the 'eternal triangle', but the wife, Clelia, is dead – hence the title – and her spirit is evoked by her husband and her lover. Svevo's interest in spiritualism, which produced its most comic result in the table-turning episode in *La coscienza di Zeno*, dates from 1913, and it is likely that this comedy belongs to that year. Clelia materializes in order to stifle nascent discord between her former husband and lover, who were good friends; but they each have their own motives for wishing to communicate with her. Her lover, an author, wants inspiration for his work, while her husband, a coffee-importer, wants to know future trends in the coffee market. Both quarrel with her and then, partly in order to satisfy their grievances against each other, and partly to annoy Clelia, they fight. This is farcical, but the characters are quite clearly, if simply, drawn, and the dialogue is handled with greater confidence than before.

Another comedy which belongs to the same period is *Atto unico*, which is almost unique among Svevo's plays in that it is the only one, apart from a brief family sketch (IV, 663–4) to be written in Triestine dialect.[6] Svevo's subject is the servant problem, but whereas in traditional treatments of this theme it is the servants who take advantage of their scarcity value to impose on their employers conditions of employment which are advantageous to themselves, in this case it is the mistress of the house – in whom it is difficult not to see a friendly caricature of the author's dynamic mother-in-law – who attempts to blackmail her domestic staff into working efficiently when she discovers that they are thieves wanted by the police. Her scheme goes wrong when she over-plays her hand, and the four servants are only too glad to surrender to the police in order to escape her tyranny.

The plays discussed so far have been for the most part brief comedies, often with satirical overtones, it is true, but unlikely to satisfy Svevo's ambition to be a serious dramatist. His first ambitious play is the three-act *Un marito*, the manuscript of which bears the date 1903. Momo sees it as having links with the novels *Una vita* (1892) and *Senilità* (1898), and suggests that it marks the end of one period of Svevo's literary career. This is misleading. The play deals with marital relationships and problems which are very different from those dealt with in the novels, and in so far as it embodies Svevo's desire to write something more substantial for the theatre it marks the development of a trend in his career as a dramatist which began with *L'avventura di Maria* – and was, in a sense, never concluded since he was dissatisfied with the dénouement of *Un marito* and tried to rewrite it in the latter years of his life. His development as a dramatist, therefore, does not run neatly parallel to his career as a novelist. I would suggest that after an initial period of interest in the theatre from 1886 to 1892, Svevo turned mainly to narrative fiction. After the failure of *Senilità* in 1898 he tried from about 1900 onwards to write plays which would match the achievement of his novels; then, probably in 1913–14, he wrote *Atto unico* as a family entertainment, as well as *Terzetto spezzato*, and returned to serious drama in the 1920s, with a final group of four plays and the revision of *Un marito*.

Marital relations are again the subject of *Un marito*, the play on which Svevo set his highest hopes and which he particularly wished to see performed. The first stage production did not in fact take place until 1961, in Trieste, although it was broadcast on the third programme of the RAI in 1960. It is often thought to be Svevo's best play in that it depicts dramatically relationships of great psychological complexity, but it is not difficult to see why he remained dissatisfied with it. Bice is the second wife of the lawyer Federico Arcetri, who killed his first wife, Clara, when he discovered that she was unfaithful. Tried for murder, he conducted his own defence and was found not guilty on the grounds that he had acted within his rights as an offended husband – although Svevo does not make the legal basis of the acquittal very clear. Clara's mother, Arianna Pareti, in search of vengeance, gives him two letters from Bice to another man which seem to prove his second wife's infidelity. No explanation is offered of how the letters came into Arianna's hands. In spite of these flaws, the first act does reveal the ambivalent nature of the love-hate relationship which links Federico and Arianna, while the opening scenes do give the spectator the impression that there is some sort of illicit relationship between Bice and Federico's friend Paolo Mansi, thus creating suspense when Arianna makes her accusations. Federico is then invited to defend a husband charged with murdering his unfaithful wife in circumstances resembling his own. This gives Federico the opportunity to assert that he feels no remorse and still maintains the husband's right to defend his honour, and also heightens the tension, albeit clumsily.

When we learn, in the second act, that Federico's clerk, Augusto, had also been betrayed by his wife, we begin to feel that so much adultery is a strain on our credulity, although we have by now also learned that Bice loves her husband and, feeling neglected, had sought merely to awaken his love by making him jealous. She easily establishes her innocence, but not before she has exposed the basic weakness of Federico's position. 'Se anche mi trovassi colpevole, non mi uccideresti!' she tells him. 'Perché mi uccideresti? Per l'onore del tuo nome! Via! Uccidere per un nome! Il nostro sangue ha importanza e corre nelle vene del più miserabile fra noi, ma il nostro nome?' (IV, *246*) [Even if you were to find me guilty, you wouldn't kill me. Why would you kill me? For the honour of your name! Come now! Kill for a name! Blood is important and flows in the veins of the most wretched among us, but our name?] In any case, she goes on, he killed Clara because he loved her, and she accuses him of not loving *her*. Federico's anger at this point seems curiously blustering. He has so far been presented as holding passionately to his notion of honour, even though the latter quality is dependent only on 'ownership' of his wife, regarded as property, but a truly passionate man would by now have killed his wife, rather than talk of the possibility of killing her if she is unable to establish her innocence.

The truth is that Federico is no longer as confident as he was that right is on his side. Arianna's presence thus provokes in him a need constantly to justify his conduct, which is why, at the end of the second act, he rather improbably has to go and explain to her why he has refrained from killing Bice. He finds her ill, however, and, seeing his present situation as a punishment for his crime, he feels the need to atone by works of compassion, especially to Arianna, and in this he is able to enlist the aid of Bice. Here we may see why Svevo remained dissatisfied with the dénouement, which is unconvincing; it also bears a generic resemblance to the situation described by Pirandello in the short story *La signora Frola e il signor Ponza, suo genero* (1915), subsequently dramatized as *Cosí è, se vi pare* (1917), one of his most characteristic plays.

If Svevo's lengthy preoccupation with *Un marito* is evidence that his plays set him formidable problems, then more evidence is provided by *La verità*, which exists in two versions, the earlier of which is entitled *La parola*. Written between 1921 and 1925, it deals with the attempts by Silvio Arcetri to explain to his wife that what appeared to be adultery on his part was merely the result of an unfortunate combination of circumstances.[7] One is left with the feeling that a wife as gullible as Fanny deserves to be deceived, although the real centre of interest is the enthusiasm with which Silvio lives out his imaginary life in retrospect, almost convincing himself of his innocence. The earlier version is marred by unnecessary complications and by inconsistency over details, all removed in the second version.

Inferiorità belongs to much the same period. This is Svevo's most powerful one-act drama. Giovanni, a valet, is persuaded by his employer's friends to pretend to rob his master, Alfredo Picchi, but the joke becomes tragedy when Giovanni, discovering that Alfredo's avarice and pique lead him to threaten to withhold his servant's savings, kills and robs him. Giovanni is a well-developed character who is unable to understand himself because his inner conflict is at the level of the unconscious. A sense of frustration caused by personality defects provokes an act of violence which is prompted more by the need for recognition and recompense than by greed. His gesture fails because it deprives him of the only relationship in which he had achieved a sense of security, leaving him alone with a sense of inferiority, which is both psychological and economic.

Svevo's final plays, *Con la penna d'oro* and *La rigenerazione*, are both more ambitious in scope. The former is unfinished. Svevo seems to have begun it in 1926 and left only a series of drafts; the text printed in the *Opera omnia* is an attempt to realize, as far as possible, Svevo's intentions – even though these were not perhaps very clearly formulated in the author's mind. The play deals with the way in which the young widow Alice is financially dependent on her wealthy cousin Alberta. Both women are attractive; Alberta is faithful to her husband, a businessman who collects prints, and Alice becomes the mistress of Sereni, an artist who had at one time made advances to Alberta and who needs a woman to inspire him. Alberta controls the weaker Alice's life and requires that she be a model of virtue. Alice vainly tries to rebel and assert her independence. 'M'hai fatto del bene ma ora basta' (IV, *382*), she cries. [You've done good to me, but now that's enough.] Circumstances and her own passive nature combine to force her back into the rut of respectability and dependence: Alberta pays her debts and arranges for her to marry Sereni, so that she has a husband, as convention demands, but she can no longer be sure that he loves her. The play lacks a dénouement, and there are strong hints in acts three and four, with Alice's references to suicide, that it was probably to be tragic; but although tragedy is a possible outcome to this study of the way in which charity can become a form of domination, with financial dependence converting love to hatred, it might well have seemed uncharacteristically melodramatic. Svevo is usually at his best when he condemns his 'heroes' to live on in the ruins of a world which has collapsed about them. This play, in fact, illustrates both the strength and the weakness of Svevo's dramas. The tortuous relationship between the cousins is well represented, but the comic nurse, Clelia, is barely credible and the tedious Telvi, deserted by his wife, is superfluous, while even the main characters find it necessary to state explicitly ideas which in the novels Svevo manages to convey more subtly, and more effectively, by implication, as when Alice remarks to Alberta that it is strange how everyone remembers from the distant past only what suits him. Similarly, Telvi comments on the rôle of sincerity in human relationships : 'Io faccio del mio meglio per non ingannare il prossimo. È vero che negli affari faccio altrimenti e che di tutta la mia vita solo gli affari vanno bene. Non farei meglio di trattare tutta la vita come se fosse un affare?' (IV, *393*) [I do my best not to deceive my neighbour. It's true I behave differently in business, and in all my life only my business is going well. Shouldn't I do better to treat the whole of my life as if it were a business deal?] Unfinished, unsatisfactory though it is, *Con la penna d'oro* will be central to any discussion of Svevo's view of the way in which money controls relationships, together with Zeno's preoccupation with money during his relationships with Carla (in *La coscienza di Zeno*) and Felicita (in *Il mio ozio*).

Montale may have been right to say of the later plays that they are more like parts of a novel adapted for the stage than plays written for the theatre.[7] *La rigenerazione* – a title given to the final play by Apollonio – is closely linked with *Umbertino*, a story which was probably intended to form part of the unfinished sequel to *La coscienza di Zeno*. Both depict the life of an elderly couple with their recently widowed daughter, whose grief the husband finds excessive, and her son, Umbertino. Like Zeno, Giovanni Chierici undergoes one of those rejuvenation operations which were fashionable for a time in the 1920s and 30s. But how is he to demonstrate the success of the operation? The only way is to show that his virility has returned, and to that end he plies the maid with drink, as a result of which they both fall into indecorous but harmless slumber. Giovanni's mixture of youth and age is grotesque, his pathetic attempt to cheat nature and the advancing years futile.

Youth, old age and the fear of death – these are the basic themes of much of Svevo's last work, and perhaps for this reason, or because they had already been developed in prose narrative, the characters of *La rigenerazione* are more carefully drawn and varied than in Svevo's other plays. Giovanni is a splendidly confused old man, and his wife, like a more mature Augusta, is essentially a companion or even a mother-figure. 'Materna' is the adjective Svevo uses to describe her in his preliminary notes (IV, *657*). Their daughter Emma is seen perpetually in an attitude of mourning, but the dénouement implies that she will marry the Zeno-like Enrico Biggioni, her late husband's best friend.

The form of *La rigenerazione* is also remarkable. It consists of three acts, the first of which is as long as the second and third together and is perhaps an indication that what we have is far from the final version. Svevo takes too long to set the scene. The first and second acts are separated by a brief dream-sequence, the second and third by an *intermezzo*. A second *sogno* concludes the play. The function of these episodes is to reveal something of the protagonist's unconscious mind. This shows Svevo struggling unhappily to move beyond naturalism, but without the skill of other dramatists of the period, such as Ibsen, Shaw and Pirandello. It shows, too, why Svevo, whose novels are so dramatic, failed to give satisfactory theatrical form to his ideas. The tension and drama of the novels derive largely from the contrast between what the characters say and what they mean, or between their intentions and their actions, between what is said and what is not said. In the plays Svevo presents us only with what is said, which is sometimes insufficient or, more frequently, excessive and lacking in subtlety. His characterization, in addition, is too often superficial, his characters too numerous. The fragments dealing with the 1914-18 war (IV, 664-6), which is the essential background of much of his mature fiction, are evidence of an inability to dramatize one of his most serious themes – war seen as a symptom of a diseased society.

Svevo was conscious of his shortcomings as a dramatist. His letter to Silvio Benco of 23 November 1895, in which he asks the critic to read and comment on an unidentified work, probably a play, laments his inability to present his ideas in a more convincing form (I, 34). Another letter, undated, to an unknown playwright, complains of the lack of lucidity in his plays (I, 56-7). He later hoped to enlist the help of Pirandello. The latter, who had not even acknowledged receipt of the copy of *La coscienza di Zeno* which Svevo had sent him, visited Trieste in 1926 in connection with a Pirandello season at the Teatro Verdi. Svevo took him by car to see the famous caves at Postumia – only to have his hopes of a confidential talk with the master shattered by the complaints of the importunate Marta Abba and by the way in which Pirandello kept up a rather commonplace conversation, treating his host as a prominent local business man rather than as a fellow author.

As a dramatist, then, Svevo faced two forms of frustration – that of the author who fails to find recognition and, worse still, that of the artist who fails to achieve satisfaction. He was at least to avoid the second of these disappointments in his narrative fiction.

3. First Narrative Fiction, 1888–92

Italian novelists, unlike their English or French counterparts, have no well-developed national tradition to which they can relate their work, for Italy has no 'great tradition' of novel-writing in the sense in which F. R. Leavis can use the phrase in relation to the English novel, only a succession of novelists, some of whom have written great novels. There are many reasons for this – the centrifugal nature of Italy's culture, with her multiplicity of cultural centres; the aulic character of her literary traditions, which attach great prestige to poetry; the relatively later rise in Italy than in England and France of the middle classes which critics customarily regard as the essential prerequisite of the rise of the novel; and the comparatively small size, until very recently, of the reading public in a country with high illiteracy figures. An aspiring Italian novelist in the late nineteenth century had only a limited choice of Italian models on which to base his style and techniques, and Svevo, with his German education and wide reading in European literature, found none of them congenial. He disliked Manzoni, and the historical novel did not appeal to him. He could not, unlike some of his Italian contemporaries, write a novel on the Risorgimento while Trieste was still under Austrian rule, part of 'unredeemed Italy'. He respected Verga, but the latter and Capuana had opened up a path which Svevo felt unable to follow. They had described in their most powerful works the peasantry of regions which he, with his urban, middle-class background, found remote. Still less could he write in the same vein as the popular De Amicis and a number of other lesser writers, who were trying to inculcate civic virtue into the Italians by recapturing the idealism which they thought had inspired the Risorgimento. The *veristi* had turned for inspiration and example to the French novelists: Svevo was to look in the same direction, but with different interests at heart and with very different results.

Svevo's earliest attempts at writing narrative fiction have not survived. Elio Schmitz's diary tells us that he was composing short stories as early as 1881, and that in March of that year he was working on a story called *Tre caratteri*, which he was thinking of offering to *L'Indi-*

pendente. Nothing seems to have come of the idea, however, and on 12 May Elio records that Ettore was dreaming of various other works which were not completed. It was not until 1888 that his first tale appeared in print. Entitled *Una lotta*, it was serialized in *L'Indipendente* on 6, 7 and 8 January. It was followed by another story with an equally violent title, *L'assassinio di Via Belpoggio*, which appeared in nine instalments in the same newspaper between 4 and 13 October 1890. Both appeared with Svevo's now customary newspaper pseudonym 'E. Samigli'.

It is presumably to the second of these stories that Svevo refers in the *Profilo autobiografico*. After mentioning the essays, he adds briefly: 'Nell'*Indipendente* pubblicò anche una lunga novella ch'egli poi ritenne di scarso interesse.' [He also published in the *Indipendente* a long *novella* which he later considered to be of little interest.] This harsh verdict on *L'assassinio* amounts to a silent repudiation of *Una lotta*, which thus escaped attention until 1971.[1] It is in fact a slight piece of work, although not without interest. Arturo Marchetti and Ariodante Chigi, poet and sportsman respectively, are both of the opinion that a young woman who lives alone and receives male visitors in her house belongs to whoever cares to take her. Both try to make Rosina, who is such a woman, their mistress. Arturo, at the age of thirty-five, feels his youth slipping away, and decides at last to enjoy life. He quarrels with his rival, who easily knocks him out – the 'lotta' of the title is thus both metaphorical and literal – and the news Arturo receives when he recovers is that Ariodante and Rosina have left the town together. He comments wryly that he ought to have foreseen this possibility. The light, humorous tone of the story contrasts surprisingly with the stark, sombre tragedies of the nearly contemporary *L'assassinio* and *Una vita*. Its chief interest lies in the way in which Svevo makes it revolve around two contrasting characters. Arturo is a weak dreamer who tries to impose on reality an interpretation it will not bear; he thus anticipates Emilio Brentani, of *Senilità*, just as Rosina anticipates Angiolina. Svevo's irony is already to be seen, operating at the expense of Arturo, who mistakenly looks upon the strong Ariodante as the personification of ineptitude. A much more mature treatment of this situation is to be found in the unfinished later story, *Orazio Cima* (III, 264–74), in which the narrator is aware of his weakness but will in the end, one suspects, take the 'strong' Cima's mistress away from him.

L'assassinio di Via Belpoggio, as the title suggests, is a murder story. It is related mainly by an omniscient narrator in the third person singular, although the central character is also used for dramatic effect as a centre of consciousness. It is divided into three sections which bear no relation to the clumsy division into nine episodes for serial publication. We are at once plunged into the thick of events. Giorgio has killed and robbed Antonio in a dark street and is fleeing to the railway station in order to make his escape to Switzerland. At this stage we learn very little about the crime, except that Giorgio has killed on a sudden impulse. Only after he has bought his ticket does he begin to hesitate; he decides not to flee and makes his way to the sordid lodgings which he shares with a certain Giovanni. There he begins to feel safe.

In the second section, Svevo tells us more about Giorgio. He is a malcontent, and something of an idler. He is of middle-class origins but has spent his inheritance and now belongs to what one could call the sub-proletariat. His life now dominated by fear and suspicion, Giorgio conceals the money. The third part of the story relates his attempts to construct, not so much an alibi as a convincing motive for his crime. He decides to say, if arrested, that he murdered for the sake of his widowed mother – only to discover, when he goes to visit her for the first time in years, that she had died a week earlier. He then panics, attracts suspicion, is arrested and confesses.

Svevo's ambitious treatment of this story of crime and punishment owes something to Dostoyevski. In the struggle for survival Giorgio is a loser and he kills Antonio more for the sake of the integration into society which he hopes money will bring than for the money itself or the comfort it will purchase. Acting on impulse, he fails to foresee that society is bound to proclaim a murderer its enemy. It is society's enmity, not remorse at his crime – which Giorgio never feels – that is his greatest punishment. He is anxious to know what other people think of his crime and then feels horror when he reads the account the newspapers give of the murder. He feels himself the isolated and misunderstood object of universal hatred. The old woman who shouts and spits at him after his arrest personifies this hatred; and in a final, vain hope of finding the harmony and comprehension he longs for, he turns to his captor, whom the reader sees as the agent of society : 'Con voce dolcissima l'uomo dal volto dolce gli chiese se stesse meglio, poi il nome. In quella faccia non vi era segno di odio o di disprezzo e Giorgio dicendo il proprio nome lo guardò fisso per non vedere la folla alla porta' (III, *240*). [In a very gentle voice the man with the kind face asked him if he were feeling better, then his name. There was no sign of hatred or contempt in that face and

Giorgio, when giving his name, stared at him so as not to see the crowd at the door.]

The irony of the tale is that Giorgio has sought harmony – the 'dolecezza' which emerges as Svevo's elusive alternative to the competitive society – in a way which threatens the security of society and so ensures his rejection. He does so because he has yielded to a sudden impulse, and in this, and in Giorgio's shrinking from the self-knowledge which his action brings, one can see Svevo's greater debt to Schopenhauer. The German philosopher had stated in *The World as Will and Representation* that murder was the supreme expression of egoism, egoism being the 'amoral force' which 'almost instinctively' makes us look on others as possible means to our ends. It also makes us devalue others: thus Giorgio considers the life of Antonio as a trifle: 'ben poca cosa lo divideva dalla proprietà assoluta di quel pacco: La vita di Antonio!' (III, 220). [only a trifle was keeping him from absolute ownership of that parcel: the life of Antonio.] The surprise which Giorgio feels at his unplanned action is also Schopenhauerian, as is the absence of remorse, for Schopenhauer had insisted that the torment of the conscience for an act committed was not remorse but pain at having known ourselves in our true being, in our will.

The story is also, in part, a study in panic. Fear prevents Giorgio from putting his escape plans into action and drives him to hide in his lodgings. Fear in the end makes him betray himself. This theme is at first woven skilfully into the story, but in the third part it to some degree distracts attention from the other themes, with the result that the character of Giorgio fails to cohere. One could also add the criticism that Svevo knows little of the world of casual labourers, and this story is the only one in which he moves into an environment with which he is unfamiliar. Perhaps Svevo intended, in describing Giorgio's background, to offer a criticism of capitalist society. If that was his intention, he failed to realize it, and it is against Giorgio that the fiercest irony is directed. Perhaps Svevo has attempted too much in a tale of only some eight thousand words, especially as the narrator has the complex task both of relating events from Giorgio's point of view and at the same time unmasking the motives of which Giorgio himself is not conscious, accusing him of self-deception and brutal egoism, and showing that his failure is the inevitable result of flaws in his personality. It may have been an awareness of these defects which led Svevo later to refer to this story so slightingly. It may also have been the need for a larger canvas which led him to write his first full-length novel.

FIRST NARRATIVE FICTION

For the publication of *Una vita* in 1892 Svevo abandoned the pseudonym which he had used in the columns of *L'Indipendente* since 1886 and used that by which he is best known. For us, the change has a symbolic value, as though the seeker has at last found his true literary identity and is able to take up and develop, in the genre in which he is to excel, themes he has so far been able only to touch in passing. Svevo is said to have begun the novel in 1887, which was one of his most active years as an essayist. Most of the writing was done in 1889, however, although his contributions to the newspaper steadily decreased in number from 1887. In 1889 he offered the novel to the Jewish publisher Treves, with the title of *Un inetto*. It was rejected, and three years later it was published by Vram of Trieste, at Svevo's expense, in a cheap edition of only one thousand copies, in crude type and on cheap paper. The title was changed at the request of the publisher, since it imprudently drew attention to a protagonist who failed signally to conform to the fashionable cult of the larger-than-life hero.

The life described in the novel is that of Alfonso Nitti. Born in the country and adored by his widowed mother, Nitti comes to Trieste in about 1880 to work as a humble clerk in the correspondence section of the Maller bank. He has a University degree in 'lettere' and is convinced of his intellectual superiority, which he attempts in vain to demonstrate. He despises the routine work of the bank, with which he is unable to cope adequately, and takes refuge in day-dreams of success, both with women and in business, and in literature and philosophy. He intends to found a new school of Italian philosophy, and sets about destroying conventional ideas of morality, but gets no further, as he is incapable of constructive thought. Meanwhile he is introduced into the Maller house, where he meets his employer's daughter Annetta. She is vain and superficial, but since she takes up literature as a pastime Nitti comes into favour. They begin to collaborate on a novel which is written in accordance with Annetta's banal ideas, which Nitti knows will be bad. He begins to play the part of Annetta's admirer. Acting on a sudden impulse, like Giorgio, he seduces her and so finds himself in a position to realize his dreams of wealth and marriage to his employer's daughter. Yet he fails to follow up this initial victory. In order to leave Trieste he invents the excuse that he must visit his sick mother – to find, when he reaches his native village, that she is dying. When he returns to Trieste he finds Annetta engaged to her cousin Macario; Nitti has been cast aside. At the bank he is demoted. He finds he is still able to browbeat

Maller into improving his position, but this victory leaves him unsatisfied. Anxious to dispel any misunderstandings there might be about his intentions, he asks Annetta to meet him. Faced with what seems to be a threat to her security, Annetta sends instead her brother, an expert duellist, who compels Nitti to challenge him. Nitti's death is inevitable; but instead of fighting he resolves to renounce wordly ambition and commits suicide.

Una vita was not a success: most of the thousand copies printed were given by Svevo to friends and acquaintances. Only three reviews, two of which appeared in Triestine newspapers, marked its publication, which passed almost unnoticed in Italy. Svevo was disappointed and claimed in later life that had it been better received he would have given up his post in the bank in order to fill in the gaps in his neglected literary education. At the same time he admitted that in *Una vita* he displayed an immaturity one might not have expected from a man in his thirties. Nor has the novel fared well at the hands of subsequent critics, at least until very recently. It is perhaps revealing – although not surprising in a first novel – that this, more than Svevo's other works, shows the influence of other novelists. He was accused of taking his title from Maupassant's *Une vie*; and his subsequent assertion that he had read all Maupassant's novels but that one is not very convincing. It has been pointed out that he owes much to Stendhal. Again, the remark that he had at this time read '... something by Stendhal' is curiously misleading. Svevo's constant attempts to cover his tracks and minimize the extent of his indebtedness to others may be in part a manifestation of his insecurity, and in part a justifiable awareness of his originality, but in this particular case it is undeniable that the characters of Nitti and Annetta and the general structure of *Una vita* owe much to the second part of *Le Rouge et le noir*. In both novels a young man of poor background is introduced into the home of his wealthy employer, whose daughter he seduces. From making that observation to pointing out that Svevo lacks Stendhal's unity and sense of purpose is a short step, and it is frequently remarked that *Una vita* lacks a focus. 'The novel is half a dozen things at once, the study of a milieu and a profession, an éducation sentimentale, a tragedy of urbanisation and a case-history, in the manner of Stendhal, of the bourgeois Napoleon-cult ... it is centrifugal without having a centre', writes Furbank.

The novel may, however, have greater unity than has so far been suggested. On to the main plot, Svevo has grafted a number of subplots, all of which are related to the main one. Nitti's seduction of

First Narrative Fiction

Annetta and the Maller family's attempts to find her a more suitable husband are paralleled by the situation in the Lanucci family, with whom Nitti lodges: Signora Lanucci would clearly like her unattractive daughter to marry Nitti, whose secure job at the bank would make him a fine catch for a working-class girl. But Nitti spurns Lucia, who is made pregnant by a suitor, Gralli, who then professes himself unable to marry the girl for financial reasons. Signora Lanucci's thoughts revert to Nitti: how splendid it would be to tell Gralli that they had found someone better – as the Maller family tells Nitti. Gralli is eventually bribed into honouring his obligations, his behaviour contrasting with that of Nitti, who rejects the chance of a wealthy marriage.

Nitti is encouraged in his love for Annetta by Francesca, who is Maller's mistress. Her ambition to marry the widower Maller is strenuously opposed by Annetta, partly out of respect for her mother's memory and partly because she sees a potential step-mother as a threat to her supremacy in the house. Francesca, believing that Annetta's opposition will collapse if she is married to Nitti, presents herself to the latter as a friend and counsellor. Finally, and less important, there is the shadowy figure of Rosina, a girl in Nitti's native village to whom he had once been attracted. She was evidently disappointed by Nitti's departure, but on his return he finds her engaged to the village shop-keeper's son. She is about to make, by local standards, a good marriage, better than she would have done had she married Nitti. It is a warning to Nitti, reinforcing that already given by Francesca, that in leaving Trieste he was losing Annetta. And as a sombre background to Nitti's emotional life, there is the bank, with its tedious routine and its bitter rivalries. Nitti's complaints about the bank begin the novel, the final words of which are 'Maller e Co'.

These sub-plots are notable both for the way in which they provide parallels or counterpoints to the main plot and for the language and imagery used to describe them. Nitti's work is not documented with the wealth of technical detail which one would expect from a thorough-going naturalist: nor is his 'ambiente' studied for its own sake. Instead, Svevo gives impressionistic glimpses of a setting which is dreary – narrow, dark corridors and gloomy offices – and a work which Nitti finds equally dreary – the accurate transcription of numbers and standardized forms of reply to business letters. Yet love – indeed, all relationships – and work are discussed in the same language. Nothing, in this bleak world, is 'given' or 'granted'; it is 'won' or 'lost'. Human beings never meet in love or friendship, only in conflict.

Svevo's novel depicts the struggle for life and stresses that the fight for survival always conditions the behaviour of men and women of all classes – peasantry and country shopkeepers, urban proletariat and middle class alike, in all circumstances.

Thus Nitti from the beginning thinks of his relationship with Annetta as a struggle. In his initial gloom he sees it as 'una lotta in cui doveva soggiacere' (II, i, *225*) [a struggle in which he was bound to succumb], and later as 'una lotta che dopo vinta bisognava sempre ricominciare' (II, i, *263*) [This struggle ... once won, would always be starting all over again], in which an embrace represents either a 'victory' for him and a 'defeat' for Annetta, or is 'revenge' for an earlier 'defeat' suffered at her hands. Francesca's advice offers a means of 'triumphing over' Annetta, of bringing to an end the 'lotta di ogni giorno nella quale si trovava da oltre un anno, lotta che aveva sempre il medesimo risultato, mai né una vittoria né una disfatta definitiva' (II, i, *284*) [the daily struggle in which he had been engaged for a year, a struggle always with the same result, neither victory nor definite defeat]. Francesca hopes to find in Nitti 'un alleato nella sua lotta alla quale anche in nome dell'onestà e della giustizia si doveva augurare la vittoria' (II, i, *343*) [an ally in the struggle which she should win in the name of honesty and justice]. So, too, at the bank, hostility is the order of the day. At first Nitti does not understand this and cannot comprehend why his colleagues become so involved in matters which he considers unimportant. Later, initiated by Annetta and Macario, he looks at them with new understanding: 'Intorno a lui, alla banca stessa, si lottava con un accanimento che gli faceva sentire meglio l'elevatezza della sua posizione, lontano da quella lotta tanto accanita, quanto meschina' (II, i, *384*). [Around him at the bank went on battles whose savagery made him realize better the superiority of his own position above such struggles, petty as they were savage.] Castris comments that in *Una vita* there is no heroism, that situations are never lived out under the banner of a lofty sentiment or a sincere faith. For this is the point of the novel. Schopenhauer and Herbert Spencer are the unnamed but unmistakably omnipresent Co-presidents of the Immortals in the world of Svevo's first fiction. The use of 'organismo' to describe the body and the frequent use of the organic analogy show how biological, in the Spencerian manner, is Svevo's approach to society and the individual. Here, too, is the link with Schopenhauer; his concept of the Will is very like a philosophical version of the biological impulse towards survival in Spencer.

But is there not some ambiguity here? Svevo's presentation of society, with competition undermining even well-established relationships, leaves no doubt that he wishes to criticize it on moral grounds; but that Nitti is the target for much of the narrator's irony rules out the straight-forward interpretation of *Una vita* offered by some critics as a study of the way in which capitalist society destroys an individual who attempts to step beyond the confines of his own class. The account of the way in which Giacomo, a fourteen-year-old boy who laughs and plays with the other lads when he first comes to the bank, is transformed into one of the most indomitable fighters, totally lacking in pity for the vanquished, recalls the essay 'Un individualista' (1886). Here Svevo compares the way in which the demands of society distort human character to the way in which rocks in the ground distort the roots of growing trees, implying once again the desirability of an alternative order. But are not rocks as 'natural' as trees? Are the rocks which impede the natural growth of the trees immoral? Can a society in which fierce competition is seen as the result of biological impulses or Schopenhauer's 'amoral force' be judged on moral grounds? Svevo was a socialist, and presumably believed that in socialism he had found a more just social order. But the story *La tribù*, of 1897, with its suggestion that society should retreat into Arcadia, indicates that Svevo recoiled from Marx's deterministic prophecies of a future in which the lot of the workers was to grow much worse before it improved, by means of a cataclysm. Spencer argued optimistically that man had now reached the stage at which he could direct his own evolution towards a better society and the cessation of conflict. In *Una vita* there are no signs of such optimism on Svevo's part. He thus presents the problem of an individual who is torn between the unscrupulous individualism of a society in which self-aggrandizement is the norm, and an ethical alternative of which hints are given in Nitti's longing for love based on harmony and his attempts to help Lucia. Nitti recoils from conflict but is too weak to achieve harmony.

One of the results of Svevo's wide-ranging interest in science and philosophy is that he is never in the position of using science in simplistic fashion as the sole or total explanation of human behaviour. He does not degrade human beings to the level of animals, as is often the case with Zola, and he is saved from pseudo-science in the manner of Capuana by his psychological insight. Svevo's message is not that individuals generally, faced with a hostile society, have no scope for action and are condemned to impotence, but that Nitti, in a society in which hostility is the norm and is accepted as such by everyone but him, is a man whose childhood and culture have left him defenceless.

With his introspective nature, his timidity and ambition, his conviction of his intellectual superiority, and his megalomaniac daydreams, Nitti is the odd man out rather than the representative of a social class. It is often remarked that Nitti's mother plays as important a part in *Una vita* as does Zeno's father in *La coscienza di Zeno*. She has shielded her son from a proper understanding of the social struggle, so that for much of the novel he is able to think of life in the country in terms more appropriate to the make-believe world of pastoral poetry than to the real world. She has, too, inhibited his emotional and sexual development, and much of the novel can be interpreted in Freudian terms, although it was written before Freud had begun to publish the results of his investigations. Nitti is bound to recoil from the prospect of marrying Annetta, perhaps from the sex act itself, because of his emotional attachment to his mother, about whom he weaves fantasies of the kind which Freud was later to call 'family romance'. He is also an angelist, divorcing love from sex and preferring to contemplate women from afar. And like Giorgio, Nitti forgets his mother for a time during the course of his affair with Annetta, only remembering her when he wants to use her as an excuse to run away. Maller in this situation becomes something of a father-figure, urging him to face up to the real world and forget the comforting dreams of childhood. It is this degree of psychological insight which is Svevo's greatest achievement in *Una vita*.

Pseudo-science is exemplified in the novel by Macario, who believes that the difference between Nitti and other people can be explained in biological terms; his brain is too well developed. Macario illustrates his argument by reference to the seagulls, all wing, eyes and stomach, so well adapted to the task of catching fish. 'Ma il cervello! Che cosa ci ha da fare il cervello col pigliar pesci? E lei che studia, che passa ore intere a nutrire un essere inutile! Chi non ha le ali necessarie quando nasce non gli crescono mai più ... Si muore precisamente nello stato in cui si nasce, le mani organi per afferrare o anche inabili a tenere' (II, i, 207). [What has brain to do with catching fish? You study, you spend hours at a desk nourishing your brain uselessly. Anyone who isn't born with the necessary wings will never grow them afterwards ... One dies in the precise state in which one is born, our hands mere organs for snatching or incapable of holding.] Svevo's careful presentation of Nitti's development makes such a view untenable, and in any case Macario is wrong about Nitti's capacity for action. He can and does act, but only in response to sudden impulses. He seduces Annetta, and even after he has lost her he is capable of brow-beating her father into making his position at the bank more tolerable. But he is unable to follow up his initial victory, like John Braine's Joe Lampton; there is something about him which makes the fruits of such victories bitter. In part it is that he wants to feel his superiority without asserting it, to win without fighting. In part it is that he longs for harmony and understanding, which he invariably imagines operating to his advantage. Faced repeatedly with the impossiblity of finding this harmony, he convinces himself that true superiority must show itself in renunciation. This is an idea which is derived from Schopenhauer, who is not named in the novel; Svevo merely describes Nitti as reading much German philosophy.

But what a difference there is between the heroic austerity of Schopenhauer's ideal and the elaborate self-deceptions of Nitti, who imagines that renunciation is a pleasant, easy road without a goal – in short, a form of self-indulgence. By the constant use of indirect free style, which enables us to see events from both Nitti's point of view and the narrator's, and by a careful process of 'distancing', which makes it clear that the narrator does not share Nitti's view, Svevo makes us aware of the gulf between reality and Nitti's dreams. He dislikes the jungle ethic of the survival of the fittest, but he has no alternative to offer except a vague Arcadian ideal which his return to the country exposes as an illusion. His every attempt to demonstrate his detachment serves only to reveal his attachment to life and its delights. When he leaves Trieste in spite of Francesca's warning that he will lose Annetta, he slips easily into the rôle of the one jilted; he 'renounces' wealth only after hearing from Francesca that he has already lost it; he gives most of his capital as a dowry for Lucia, only to squeeze out of his generosity the last drop of gratification; and even when he imagines death, it is in terms which seem to derive directly from Petrarch's 'Chiare, fresche e dolci acque', for he sees it as a means of winning Annetta's love. This we can hardly believe. Her vanity and heartlessness have already been revealed, and so Nitti's death unites the themes of 'sogno', or illusion, and 'renunciation', which have in common the element of self-deception. Had Nitti read his Schopenhauer more carefully, he would have realized, as Svevo did, that the philosopher did not consider suicide as a form of renunciation, since he stated that: 'Far from being denial of the will, suicide is a phenomenon of the will's strong affirmation. For denial has its essential nature in the fact that the pleasures of life, not its sorrows, are shunned. The suicide wills life, and is dissatisfied merely with the conditions on which it has come to him.'[2] And in case the elaborate self-deceptions of the final paragraphs of the novel, narrated from Nitti's point of view, are not enough to expose the inadequacy of this 'via di divenire superiore ai sospetti e agli odii' (II, i, *425*) [way to become superior to other's suspicions and hatreds], Svevo ends the novel with a letter from the bank to Nitti's guardian containing the bleak comment: 'Vi annunciamo che ci sono del tutto ignote le cause che spinsero al suicidio il nostro impiegato Signor Alfonso Nitti' (II, i, *426*). [We would inform you that the reasons for which our clerk Alfonso Nitti committed suicide are quite unknown.]

Una vita undoubtedly has its faults. In the opening chapters we are presented in too brief a space of time with a bewilderingly large gallery of minor characters, and the techniques which Svevo uses to introduce and describe them are limited and tend to become monotonous. And as we shall see in a later chapter, Svevo's irony can find only a limited number of ways of expressing itself. Francesca, on whom much of the action depends, is too shadowy a figure, and Annetta seems to be an attempt to personify the literary cliché of the woman whose cold exterior conceals a sensual and passionate nature. Perhaps the most serious criticism of the novel is that whereas the psychological causes of Nitti's failure are analysed with insight, the language and imagery of Svevo's account of society and the social struggle are repetitive. Thus there is a certain diffuseness about the narrative which is not due to the complexity of Svevo's themes but to his inability to communicate his vision of society in a more concentrated fashion. It is this which has led to the inaccurate charge that *Una vita* is 'centrifugal without having a centre'. The vision is there; the failure is purely technical.

Even with these faults, *Una vita* is a remarkable first novel. It has some delightful satirical touches and, more importantly, there is a maturity of psychological insight in Svevo's account of Nitti's life and a breadth of vision about his presentation of society at different levels which enable him to introduce many of the themes which will recur in his mature narrative work.

4. *Senilità*, 1898

By the time *Una vita* appeared in 1892, or very shortly after, Svevo was at work on his second novel. In 1897 he chose its title, and in 1898 it was serialized in *L'Indipendente* – *Una vita* probably having been considered too long for publication in that form – and it appeared in book form in the same year, published by Vram of Trieste in a cheap edition of one thousand copies. In every way this second novel is an improvement on the first, and some Italian critics have considered it Svevo's finest novel. Montale, for example, found it his most artistically satisfying book. Some, like Battaglia, still prefer it to *La coscienza di Zeno*, and even though contemporary critical opinion does on the whole prefer the latter novel, one nevertheless must recognize that *Senilità* is a masterpiece, an outstanding example of psychological analysis and of the 'well-made novel' in the eulogistic sense in which J. Warren Beach uses the phrase in *The Twentieth-Century Novel* (1923).

Svevo's central character is Emilio Brentani, a minor employee with a Triestine insurance company. He comes of a family which has seen better days – a *motif* to be found in *L'assassinio di via Belpoggio* and *Una vita* – but he earns enough to support himself and his sister Amalia, and he has no great social ambitions. He is the author of a now unread novel, a fact which confers on him a rather spurious local prestige. The narrator's account of Brentani's novel, concerning the merits of which the author himself has no illusions, makes it sound curiously like one of the then popular novels of Verga's 'second manner', such as *Tigre reale* (1873), on which Svevo had commented so harshly in his essay on *Mastro-Don Gesualdo*. There is an undercurrent of literary satire in *Senilità* comparable to that in *Una vita*.

Brentani, like Arturo Marchetti, has lived a cautious life. He is, he has told himself, responsible for his sister, and so, 'sentendosi le spalle gravate di tanta responsabilità, egli traversava la vita cauto, lasciando da parte tutti i pericoli ma anche il godimento, la felicità' (II, i, 433) [acting as if this weight of responsibility obliged him to go cautiously through life, avoiding all its perils, but also its pleasures and all hope of earthly felicity]. Now, at the surely symbolic age of thirty-five – 'nel mezzo del cammin di *sua* vita' – he finds 'nell'anima la brama insoddisfatta di piaceri e di amore, e già l'amarezza di non averne goduto, e nel suo cervello una grande paura di se stesso e della debolezza del proprio carattere, invero piuttosto sospettata che saputa per esperienza' (ibid.). [The desire for pleasures he had never tasted, for love he had never known surged up in his heart, but with a sense of bitterness and frustration at the thought of all he might have enjoyed; and he was conscious at the same time of a great mistrust of himself, and of the weakness of his own character which hitherto he had had occasion to suspect rather than to prove by actual experience.] He has so far been able to live out his adventures in the security of his imagination; in this way, as the narrator later tells us, 'Del delinquente aveva sentito il coraggio e la forza e la perversità ... Ma poi, soddisfatto dal sogno, egli aveva ritrovato immutati gli oggetti che aveva voluto distruggere, e s'era chetato, la coscienza tranquilla' (II, i, 455). [He had experienced imaginatively the criminal's courage, strength and perverse desires ... But then he had had the double satisfaction of indulging in his dream and of discovering all the things he had wanted to destroy still intact, so that his senses were satisfied and his conscience at rest.] So long as these impulses can be confined within the safe limits of his dream world, no real harm is done. The novel begins at the moment at which Brentani's dissatisfaction leads him to embark on a love affair, in order to live out a dream and experience the joys of love before it is too late, thus disturbing the delicate equilibrium between his humdrum daily life and his fantasy world, and between what the narrator calls his 'two careers', his petty job and his literary ambition. He proposes to act out the novel he can no longer write, confusing art and life.

The object of Brentani's desires is Angiolina Zarri, a young and beautiful working-class girl, apparently shy and innocent, whose acquaintance he has casually made in the park. The situation is fraught with paradox and pregnant with possibilities of irony. It is hinted from the beginning that Angiolina is not all she seems, that it was she, not Brentani, who took the initiative in bringing about their meeting. Brentani, on his side, not only proceeds on the assumption that she is the innocent creature that his Don Giovanni pose demands that she be, but he specifically asks of her only facile pleasure without emotional commitment. This, it turns out, is the only kind of love Angiolina has to offer. For the sake of his adventure Brentani has temporarily adopted the moral values of young men-about-town, represented in the novel by such minor characters as Bardi, Carlini,

Leardi and Sorniani, thus stifling what he later claims to be one of the deepest impulses of his nature, namely a longing for 'dolcezza', for harmony and understanding.

A number of critics, including Battaglia and Maxia, have compared *Senilità* to a scientific experiment. Brentani has achieved a certain stability, based on resignation, compromise and self-deception. He is still able to believe that his best work as a writer is yet to come – an illusion which he preserves intact by not writing. His sister selflessly looks after him in a domestic situation which enables him to believe he has devoted his life to her. And he has the friendship of the sculptor Stefano Balli, a relationship in which he is content to be dominated. It is as though Svevo had created this static situation in order to see what would happen if, to use the analogy of the experiment, a catalyst were introduced. Angiolina is the catalyst; remaining unchanged herself, she provokes disastrous changes in others. Brentani is of course the principal reagent, but not the principal victim. If, as some critics have complained, Svevo introduces his main characters too quickly, it is because of the need to set up the experiment as quickly as possible.

The structure and techniques of the novel all derive naturally and economically from this initial situation. *Una vita* began with Nitti's move to Trieste and his employment at the Maller bank; it surveyed the Triestine social scene at different levels; it introduced in so doing a host of minor characters whose relevance was not always clear; and it moved through time in linear fashion, albeit at varying speeds and with occasional halts. There is no attempt in *Senilità* to survey different milieux in the same way; Svevo is content simply to indicate clearly but unobtrusively the social and economic status of his characters by suggestion and implication. Whereas we needed to see Nitti at work in order to trace the development of his attitude to the struggle for life, we do not need to see Brentani in his office since our attention is directed to his fantasy life, which finds no expression at work. We consequently have a much more restricted group of minor characters, all of whom have a small but useful part to play. We have, moreover, not one principal character but four, and the novel is based on a series of contrasts and analogies between them. They are presented singly, or in twos or threes in a variety of combinations, but never all four together; since Amalia is a respectable middle-class woman, and Angiolina deserves neither of these epithets, they cannot in the 1880s be allowed to meet. Svevo turns this apparent restriction to good use, however, for Brentani, in talking to his sister about his beloved, is free to weave his fantasies about her unchecked. Three characters, moreover, are used as centres of consciousness through whom alternative points of view can be offered; Angiolina is rarely, if ever, used in this way. Thus the narrator, after the initial pages, seldom needs overtly to interpose his judgement between the reader and his characters. He can limit himself on the whole to defining or explaining, and his attitude towards Brentani consequently appears – but only appears – to be less harsh than it was to Nitti. Finally, *Senilità* lacks the earlier novel's linear structure; it has instead a remarkable circular quality. In part this is because time in the second novel is treated as a more subjective factor and is therefore more fluid; in part it is the inevitable result of Brentani's principal characteristic.

Flaubert's Emma Bovary is frequently mentioned as one of Brentani's chief precursors, as indeed she is. Svevo greatly admired *Madame Bovary*, which he described in 1890 as an earthquake shock, the effects of which could still be felt in Italian literature. There is, however, an important difference between the two characters. Emma Bovary's tragedy was that she attempted consistently to live out one dream, that of romantic love; she cast herself and her lover into rôles which took no account of a reality which inevitably asserted its claims. Brentani's *Bovarysme* is of a different kind. He too assigns rôles – to Angiolina, that of innocence, which is a cliché suggested by her radiant health and his lack of literary talent, for as the narrator points out, rhetoricians always assume that good health and corruption are incompatible. He sees himself at first as a kind of 'homme fatale', and when he kisses her in the moonlight, he feels more deliciously wicked than ever: 'Baciava la bianca, casta luce' (II, i, 445) [He was kissing the pure virginal moonlight]; but he is never able to stay for long in one pose.

He is easily able to accommodate to this fantasy world the rumours which soon begin to reach him about Angiolina's past, but when irrefutable evidence of her deceptions is presented, he finds himself trapped between the declared cynicism of his intentions and the truth of an emotional involvement which is deeper than he had intended. Angiolina, he realizes, can satisfy him physically but not emotionally, and he angrily gives her up. As he does so, he reveals his inner contradictions:

... io le ho voluto bene e per questo solo fatto avevo il diritto di essere trattato altrimenti. Quando una ragazza permette ad un giovane di dirle di amarla, ella è già sua e non più libera. – Questa frase era debole ma molto esatta, in un rimprovero amoroso

SENILITÀ

anche troppo. Infatti egli non aveva altro diritto al quale appellarsi che il fatto di averle detto d'amarla (II, i, 495). [I loved you very much and that alone ought to have given me the right to be treated differently. When a girl allows a young man to tell her he loves her she belongs to him and is not free to do as she likes. This phrase was rather feeble, but it expressed exactly what he wanted to say, which is a great deal to expect of a lover's reproach. He had in fact no other claim to plead save the fact that he had told her he loved her.]

It is inconsistent of Brentani to complain that Angiolina had given him only what he initially asked for. D.J. Enright has complained of Svevo's heroes that they are all potential slave-owners, which is a perceptive comment;[1] Svevo is making Brentani unconsciously talk of love in terms of the Hegelian master-slave relationship which is already implicit in his initial treatment of Angiolina as what one might now call a sex object. He then leaves before Angiolina has time to ask what rights he had over her – a departure which the narrator presents as a flight from danger.

Brentani is then forced to recognize that he has idealized Angiolina into something she was not – an idealization epitomized by the nickname of *Ange* which he gives her. There has been no deception on her part, except in so far as she had tried to react in accordance with what she had vaguely guessed to be his wishes. But she had found this process tiring, since Brentani had been in turn cynical seducer, worldly-wise educator and lyrical lover ready to lose all for love. She was unable to keep up with his changes of rôle. 'Oh, ella non sapeva fingere. La donna ch'egli amava, *Ange*, era sua invenzione, se l'era creata lui con uno sforzo voluto; essa non aveva collaborato a questa creazione, non l'aveva neppure lasciato fare perché aveva resistito. Alla luce del giorno il sogno scompariva' (II, i, 459). [No, she was incapable of deceit. The woman he loved, *Ange*, was his own invention, he had created her by an effort of his own will : Angiolina had had no part in this creation, she had even, by the resistance she had offered, prevented its completion. The dream vanished in the light of day.] *Sogno*, *sognare* and *sognatore* are regularly recurring key words in *Senilità*.

The rupture in chapter VII is inevitable. Three chapters, nearly a fifth of the novel's length, and an undetermined period of time later, Brentani sees Angiolina again in the street. Her shoes shine in the lamp-light – an interesting piece of fetishism which makes one suspect an elment of masochism in his nature – and his desire for her is as sharp as ever. They take up where they left off and the cycle is ready to repeat itself, this time with tragic consequences. Before we can consider the rest of the affair, however, we must examine the other main characters.

There are two main lines of interpretation of *Senilità*. Some critics – Maier, Jonard and Furbank, for example – see the main characters of the novel as dividing neatly into two pairs, one of which is 'senile', the other 'healthy', with Brentani and his sister standing in sharp contrast to Angiolina and Balli. Others – for example, Saccone and Gatt-Rutter – argue that all four suffer in varying degrees from *senilità*, which has been defined as 'an inability to realize positive human values' and as a lack of a 'grip on reality'. The 'senile' character takes refuge in day-dreams and illusions which he tries to impose on reality. 'Imagery' is the name which R. Pfohl has given to this disease.

Brentani is undoubtedly the 'senile' character *par excellence*, and his sister seems to match him perfectly. She is older than her brother, a desiccated spinster whose life has known no joy; she is described in terms of colourlessness, and of blacks and greys, both contrasting with the light, the gold and the warm colours with which Angiolina is associated. When love enters her brother's life, it changes her existence too. Brother and sister embark on the same adventure, since she listens eagerly to all he has to tell her of Angiolina. In consequence she feels abandoned; she comes to understand her brother's lack of concern for her and to know that her life lacks love, and that love can be a source of joy. Her tragedy is that she has a capacity for love which no one wants.

As Brentani dreams by day, so his sister, in love with Balli, dreams by night. When Brentani realizes this, he finds an excuse to exclude his friend from their house, and his consequent sense of guilt at having deprived Amalia of her one source of happiness creates yet another barrier between brother and sister. But as well as an analogy there is also a contract between the two, for Amalia's initial reaction to Balli's absence is seen even by Brentani to be more courageous than that of her brother to his separation from Angiolina. He responds to her heroism merely by formulating vague resolutions to devote himself to her future. Her subsequent alcoholism exposes more effectively than any direct authorial comment the ineffectiveness of Brentani's resolution.

The pages describing Amalia's delirium and death are very powerful. They recall the account of Signora Nitti's death in *Una vita*, but are more relevant to the novel's meaning in *Senilità*. Amalia lies dying, loved at last by Balli, ironically enough, with the highest love of which he is capable – that of the artist for an intense visual experience. Svevo is thus able to imply both that Amalia is unlovable and that Balli is incapable of true love. At that point Brentani chooses to go to see Angiolina for the last time. He assumes for the occasion a pose of superior, ironical detachment; how wrong, he reflects, he and Amalia had been to take life so seriously. He then wanders down to the harbour, where he sees a sailor make a boat secure against the storm that is raging; projecting his own emotions into the violent sea-scape he sees himself as the passive and helpless victim of circumstances. The lyricism of this and a few other passages has led a number of readers to assume that at moments like this Brentani achieves a new understanding of himself. This is not the case. This episode is narrated consistently from Brentani's point of view, and in it he is attempting to absolve himself of all responsibility for the harm he has done. Svevo's central characters are determinists when it suit thems to be. The falsity of his pose, however, is revealed by the disproportion between Brentani's posturing and Amalia's real tragedy; Svevo inflates the lyricism of his description until it becomes a criticism of the character and exposes him as morally reprehensible.

Amalia dies twice – once literally, and the second time metaphorically, in her brother's memory, when, in the final paragraphs of the novel, some of her characteristics are incorporated into the new idealized image of Angiolina which Brentani constructs in retrospect. James Joyce, who suggested the title of the English translation of *Senilità* (*As a Man Grows Older*), learned this passage off by heart as an example of fine style. But as in the storm scene, lyricism here is neither an end in itself nor merely the appropriate form in which to express an emotional experience which Svevo expects us to find moving. That Amalia should be forgotten so easily is offensive, and Brentani is thereby condemned. At the same time this ending, in view of Amalia's total lack of self-assertiveness, is ironically appropriate.

Amalia is a victim of her social situation and even of literature. She has been pressed, to the exclusion of all else, into the rôle of housekeeper, and even in her delirium she is preoccupied with details of housekeeping. Love is all the more devastating because it has always been presented to her as something forbidden, and she has known it only in the pages of the hundreds of novels in the Brentani book-case, each of which she has read. Has she not read far too many novels? One is reminded that Madame Bovary senior wanted to cancel her daughter-in-law's subscriptions to a circulating library. Svevo is not saying, any more than was Flaubert, that literature is by its nature liable to corrupt, but that in the absence of real love the attempt to live out an unreal fiction can have tragic consequences. Both authors imply that most novels, however, have no basis in real life and so are dangerous.

Balli certainly has his virtues: he is, for example, more capable of compassion than Brentani, but on closer consideration he, too, turns out to be a failure. His artistic *credo* has been the subject of some discussion, with De Castris asserting that his ideal of '... spontaneità ... ruvidezza voluta ... semplicità ...' to express 'il suo "io" artistico depurato da tutto ciò ch'era idea o forma altrui' (II, i, 438) [spontaneity, a certain wilful ruggedness, a simplicity ... his artistic 'ego' ... purified of all that was not original either in form or idea] is an expression of Svevo's aesthetic. One could go back to Svevo's 1887 essay *Del sentimento in arte* to show that this is a naïvely romantic ideal which Svevo had already rejected, and the constant use in the novel of 'diceva' and 'credeva' shows that the narrator is being careful not to associate himself with Balli's views. Svevo then goes on to show that Balli had consistently failed to give adequate expression to his ideas. His studio is full of abandoned projects and his failure is made more pointed by his inability to finish the projected statue of Angiolina, the inspiration for which is literary rather than sculptural. Balli is often said to have been modelled on Svevo's friend Umberto Veruda, the Triestine post-impressionist painter, but whereas Svevo admired Veruda he described Balli in his correspondence as not very artistic. I doubt whether Balli owes to Veruda anything more than a few superficial mannerisms: he may owe much more to Svevo's interest in such sculptors as Salvatore Grita, whose *Polemiche artistiche* he had reviewed in 1884, and Lorenzo Bartolini, the Florentine sculptor, to whom he refers in *Del sentimento in arte*, whose polemical attitudes earned him great unpopularity and recall Balli's.

Nor can Balli be said to be any less of a failure in his personal relationships. Whenever he is seen as strong and attractive, it is always through the eyes of another character who is dominated by him – Brentani, Amalia or Angiolina. 'Il Balli era la virtù e la forza' (II, i, 476) [It was Balli who stood for virtue and strength], for example, is the reaction of the infatuated Amalia, as is the later comment: 'Come era bello il destino del Balli ...' (ibid. p. 478) [What a splendid destiny Balli's seemed.] Balli, in fact, is friendly only with people whom he

SENILITÀ

can dominate. This is true particularly of his friendships with women, which he exploits in order to compensate for his failure as an artist. He resents the 'intrusion' of Angiolina, whom he sees as a threat to his relationship with Brentani, and in his way he is as dependent on the latter as Brentani is on him. He is, moreover, an egoist with an arrogantly high opinion of himself. It is true that he feels sorry for his friend, but his insensitive attempts to help him are disastrous. He is too preoccupied with his own wit, for example, to notice the effect on Brentani of his account of Angiolina's infidelity with the umbrella-man, and his belief that his friend is 'cured' of his infatuation is prompted mainly by his desire to use Angiolina as a model. His friendship for Brentani is thus undermined by his art, just as Brentani's affection for him is undermined by jealousy and resentment.

His chief failure, in other words, is to see people as individuals. To him they are objects to be judged in terms of shape and colour and of his aesthetic reactions to them – hence his initial reaction to the sight of Angiolina with Brentani or with the umbrella-man. This trait is to be seen most clearly in his attitude to Amalia: it is he who reflects that she was born grey. Yet he can fight for her attention without noticing the effect he is having on her. Svevo refrains from pointing the moral, but there is little difference in kind, only in intensity, between the way in which Balli holds up lighted matches to compare the faces of Angiolina and Margherita, the way he watches the dogs that are to be put down, and the way he contemplates the dying Amalia. He reduces everything to the level of a visual experience. The chief difference between Brentani and Balli is that the latter has only fleeting glimpses of his personal inadequacies and, with his customary facility in explaining everything, he always succeeds in explaining them away. The main function of the superficial differences between them is to highlight their fundamental similarity.

Since Angiolina is seen mainly through the eyes of Brentani and Balli, she is consistently described as beautiful and alluring, 'il volto illuminato dalla vita, un color giallo di ambra soffuso di rosa da una bella salute' (II, i, 434) [her face glowing with life, an amber suffused with the pink of splendid health], her beauty and capacity for sexual pleasure contrasting with that of Amalia, her health and youth with Brentani's 'sickness' and 'senilità'. She does not understand her lover. She sometimes tries to conform to the pattern of behaviour which she thinks he expects of her, and much of the black comedy of the novel derives from her failure to do so. Indeed, how could she succeed? Not only is her understanding limited by her boundless vanity, but she and Brentani do not share the same values. His are those of his Utopian dream-world; hers are those of the men-about-town to whom she sells her love. It is typical of both characters that Angiolina asks for money so charmingly that Brentani does not realize the implications of her doing so. Her piety is false, her vulgarity, which she makes no attempt to conceal, is real. She is appalled by Brentani's idealized account of the future socialist society in which wealth will be equally shared, for if all have equal shares, where will she find her rich lovers? Nor is she moved by his account of the astronomer and his beloved living in amorous isolation in their mountain-top observatory, since she needs the constant reassurance of other men's admiring glances.

Are her health and youth not mere physical characteristics? She lies, she sells herself. She admires Brentani only when he behaves, by his standards, despicably; first when he takes her by force, and secondly when he deceives her official fiancé Volpini into continuing their engagement. Even so, she is not to be explained solely in terms of vice; if she is not Brentani's *Ange*, neither is she the extrovert pleasure-seeker whom Balli nicknames *Giolana*, and Brentani's explanation – heredity – although partly borne out by her sister's precocious behaviour – is too simplistic to be acceptable. Svevo avoids an explicit condemnation; instead, he gives her a working-class background and a grotesque father who is even more of a failure than Lanucci in *Una vita* and whose persecution complex leads him to externalize the causes of his failure in the imaginary creatures Tic and Tac who follow him wherever he goes. Angiolina thus seeks security in money, and in order to obtain it she barters the only asset she has – her body – in a trade which is sanctioned by the group in which she moves. That in doing so she also finds sexual gratification does not mean that the pursuit of pleasure is her sole aim. Her elopement with an embezzling bank clerk epitomizes her failure to achieve even her limited ambitions, for what security has she achieved in flight with a criminal?

Angiolina's flight brings to an end the second part of her affair with Brentani, who attributes to it an almost symbolic quality, as though life itself were fleeing from him – a suggestion which Moravia was to make explicit in *La noia*, in which Dino comes to look on his elusive mistress as 'Cecilia or reality'. It also offers a contrast with the way in which, at the end of the first part, Brentani had left her. At this point the remarkable structure of the novel becomes apparent. It too, like the characterization, depends upon a series of parallels and contrasts and is much more innovatory in its technique than appears at first sight.

The account of the first stage of the affair, from the first meeting until Brentani's attempt to renounce Angiolina, occupies chapters I to VI and the first part of chapter VII. The period of time covered by these chapters is roughly three months. The novel was originally to have been called *Il carnevale di Emilio*, and it begins at Carnival-time, that is January-February of one year, probably 1882, and chapter VI takes us up to early January of the following year. But time, in *Senilità*, is more frequently measured in subjective terms, and one is surprised by Maxia's comment on what he sees as the strict realism with which time is measured, since it is seldom 'measured'; Svevo is much more concerned to communicate a sense of the speed with which time appears to his characters to pass. In the statement 'Angiolina lo fece attendere mezz'ora, un secolo' (II, i, 534) [Angiolina made him wait more than half an hour, a century], both objective and subjective notations are given at once, but the 'mesi prima' (II, i, 568) [months ago] of Brentani's uncertainty as to when he last really saw his sister is purely subjective. Chapters VII to IX cover a period of two or three weeks at the most, during which the action is static; Forti speaks of this section as a 'central stasis', and it is analogous to that section of *Una vita* in which Nitti retreats to his native village. Yet this section of the novel seems to cover a long period, mainly because it appears so to Emilio and his sister, who fall quickly into monotonous habits which are described by verbs in the imperfect tense with adverbs of time such as 'molto spesso', 'talvolta', 'mai'.

In chapter X Brentani, believing himself to be cured, tries to write a novel about his love for Angiolina, but nothing in it rings true. His heroine lacks even the life of the fashionable tiger-woman of his first novel; truth is stranger than fiction. Reality, in fact, never ceases to surprise Brentani, because he is rarely prepared for it. Tragedy, on the other hand, leaves him unharmed because, as Gatt-Rutter points out, he enjoys imagining it so much. He is therefore surprised to meet Angiolina again, surprised at the ease with which she becomes his mistress, and painfully surprised once more by her vulgarity and lies. The novel then moves swiftly to its climax. Chapters X to XIII cover a period of perhaps two months, at the end of which Brentani again renounces Angiolina and Amalia dies, a victim of alcoholism. In that brief period, the pattern of events in the first part is repeated at greater speed, with a series of carefully placed references back to the first part. In both parts Brentani begins by idealizing Angiolina, only to be disillusioned by reality. In the first part he realizes that she had been taught to kiss; in the second he is made to realize that she is more expert than he in sexual matters and that his performance in bed does not come up to the standards to which she is accustomed. In both parts he is jealous of Balli, who in the first part wishes to use Angiolina as a model and in the second does so. The supper-party in the first part has its counterpart in the second in the evening spent at the hostelry drinking mulled wine, the pleasure of which is destroyed for Brentani when he is forced to recognize that he owes Angiolina's docility to the influence of Balli. In both parts Brentani affects an indifference or detachment he is far from feeling; in both he narcissistically makes nature mirror his emotions. In both he is involved in the deception which Angiolina practises on Volpini, and despises himself for it.

Underlying these parallels, however, there is a difference. We have seen that when love entered his life it also entered his sister's. When Brentani broke with Angiolina for the first time, he also severed Amalia's only link with Balli by asking the sculptor not to visit them on the pretext, which Balli recognizes as a lie, that his sister and his friend were the subject of gossip. Amalia bears her lonely grief with heroic fortitude for a time but then succumbs to the alcoholism which accelerates and makes fatal her final illness. Amalia's tragedy is real, her fate truly moving, and it is in the perspective established by her real distress that we see and judge Emilio's posturings.

Brentani's final encounter with Angiolina fails to follow the pattern he had chosen for it; her transparent eagerness to betake herself to another rendezvous makes him lose his temper, jolting him out of his pose. Her last gesture, in pretending to faint in order to escape his grasp, is a lie, and he is denied his final satisfaction, the calm parting in which he had intended to demonstrate his superiority. But neither this episode, nor Amalia's death, as quiet and unobtrusive as her life had been, provides the note on which Svevo wishes to end his novel.

Amalia is tended in her illness by a neighbour, Signora Chierici, who has seemed to some to be one of Svevo's least satisfactory creations. He undeniably strains our credulity too far in making her the only member in Trieste of the Deluigi family for which Angiolina claimed to work, thus revealing the extent to which her life had been a tissue of lies. But this is only one of her functions. Gatt-Rutter suggests that her name associates her with the clergy and he is right to point out that she comes to Brentani *from above*, precisely at a moment when, on the landing, he used to look *down* to watch for Angiolina's approach. Signora Chierici is an assertion by Svevo that the characters he has depicted do not represent his ideal of conduct, and that disinterested virtue exercised on behalf of others is still possible in this world. She reinforces this message when Brentani calls on her some time after Amalia's funeral. Her behaviour in widowhood implies that grief for the dead can be a form of self-indulgence and she speaks from experience when she says that the living have a greater claim on our compassion. Brentani characteristically agrees, but promptly lapses into a new dream, and one this time that cannot be disturbed by the claims of reality.

Brentani finds once again the stability and security he had enjoyed at the beginning of the novel; the wheel has gone full circle. The difference is that he now has the memory of a love affair to look back on.

Anni dopo egli s'incantò ad ammirare quel periodo della sua vita, il più importante, il più luminoso. Ne visse come un vecchio del ricordo della gioventù. Nella sua mente di letterato ozioso, Angiolina subì una metamorfosi strana. Conservò inalterata la sua bellezza, ma acquistò anche tutte le qualità d'Amalia che morì in lei una seconda volta. Divenne triste, sconsolantemente inerte, ed ebbe l'occhio limpido ed intellettuale. Egli la vide dinanzi a sè come su un altare, la personificazione del pensiero e del dolore e l'amò sempre, se amore è ammirazione e desiderio. Ella rappresentava tutto quello di nobile ch'egli in quel periodo avesse pensato ed osservato.

Quella figura divenne persino un simbolo. Ella guardava sempre dalla stessa parte, l'orizzonte, l'avvenire da cui partivano i bagliori rossi che si riverberavano sulla sua faccia rosea, gialla e bianca. Ella aspettava! L'immagine concretava il sogno ch'egli una volta aveva fatto accanto ad Angiolina e che la figlia del popolo non aveva compreso (II, i, 594–5).

[Years afterwards he looked back with a kind of enchanted wonder on that period, which had been the most important and the most luminous in his life. He lived on it like an old man on the memories of his youth. Angiolina underwent a strange metamorphosis in the writer's idle imagination. She preserved all her own beauty, but acquired all the qualities of Amalia, who died a second time in her. She grew sad and dispirited, her eye acquired an intellectual clarity. He saw her before him as on an altar, the personification of thought and suffering, and he never ceased loving her, if admiration and desire are love. She stood for all that was noble in his thought and vision during that period of his life.

Her figure even became a symbol. It was always looking in the same direction, towards the horizon, the future from which came those glowing rays, reflected in rose and amber and white upon her face. She was waiting! The image embodied the dream he had once dreamed at Angiolina's side, which that child of the people could not understand.]

Svevo has skilfully prepared us to accept this apotheosis. Brentani had earlier imagined that the memory of him might one day ennoble Angiolina; later, when alone, he had reflected that Angiolina had influenced his sister's fate. Amalia, too, in her conversations with her brother, had contributed towards the idealization of Angiolina into *Ange*. We have known for some time that one of Brentani's characteristics was that he delighted in evoking the sentiment of the past, and we see the process at work when, after Amalia's death, he had remembered her not as she was on her death-bed, but sad and lonely when deprived of Balli's company – a memory which was also to some extent a reproach since it was he who was responsible for the situation. And when he had broken off his affair with Angiolina for the first time he had consoled himself with the thought that at least he was no longer ridiculous and that she might perhaps remember one day the man who had loved her so dearly. The way in which a man can transform his past in order to absolve himself of guilt and exorcise disturbing memories, one of the central themes of *La coscienza di Zeno*, is clearly present in *Senilità* too.

That the new Angiolina should gaze so steadfastly towards a red horizon, symbol of a socialist future, raises the question of Svevo's political beliefs and the part which they play in his novels. Svevo was a Socialist. He had read Marx and other Socialist writers, and was aware of the links between Darwinism and Marxism. That his Socialism was unorthodox is shown by the short story *La tribù*, which was published in Turati's review *Critica sociale* in 1897. It describes the way in which a hitherto nomadic tribe settles, acquires land, laws and a class structure. A certain Achmed is sent to Europe to study the laws of other countries, only to find on his return that his land has been occupied by others. Perhaps this is intended to illustrate the workings of *laissez-faire* capitalism. Hussein, the tribe's leader, offers to compensate him if he can tell the tribe, who now have too many laws, of a happier way of life. Achmed, who wants to set up a factory, explains to them the Marxist version of history in terms of class conflict, increasing misery for the workers and eventual, but distant, Utopia. Achmed is given his compensation, but he is driven out; a political philosophy based upon the assumption of increasing misery for the masses is of no use to the tribe or, apparently, to Svevo, whose humanitarianism makes him ask why we should tolerate the progressive deterioration of society if it is to result in tragedy, instead of setting about the task of reforming it. Svevo rejects a philosophy of history which seems to him to have petrified into a form of determinism, but he does not seem to be in a position to offer a clear alternative at this stage, other than a withdrawal into Arcadia. One wonders whether he had read William Morris's *News from Nowhere* (1891), with which *La tribù* has affinities.

One must not, however, over-emphasize the economic aspects of social criticism in Svevo. His protagonists are not mere stock representatives of a lower bourgeoisie whose individuality is crushed by the capitalist system. It is true that Svevo always takes care to indicate the social and economic standing of his characters, plainly in *Una vita* and discreetly in *Senilità*, and that money frequently plays a part in their relationships. Svevo is implying that given the competitive nature of society, and what he sees as exploitation, relationships tend to be dehumanized. To this extent his diagnosis is Marxian, but it is not solely Marxian in origin. He describes life in terms of conflict, and the language and imagery with which he does so derive from Spencer and Darwin; competitiveness has its origin for Svevo in a biological impulse, and this, too, is a factor which impedes the development of human relationships. Psychological factors also play a part; Nitti and Brentani encompass their own defeats, assisted by their personality defects, more than they succumb to a socio-economic system, and Svevo does not suggest that if the system were changed there would be no more psychological problems. All this amounts to a complex picture of an alienation which has a multiplicity of causes. And the protagonists themselves, as much as the society they live in, are equally the target of Svevo's criticism.

Brentani is certainly a Socialist, but his political views turn out on closer inspection to be yet another manifestation of his personal inadequacies. When he explains his Socialist ideals and his views on the equality of the sexes to Angiolina (in terms which derive from F. A. Bebel's *Die Frau und der Sozialismus* (1879)), he blames society for their misfortunes and uses his distant Utopia as a pretext for not offering to commit himself to Angiolina then and there, as Svevo's vocabulary makes clear.

Fu un sogno ch'egli ebbe e sviluppò accanto ad Angiolina e ad onta di questa vicinanza. Essi erano tanto infelici causa il turpe stato sociale vigente. Egli ne era tanto convinto che poté pensare di essere persino capace di un'azione eroica pel trionfo del socialismo. Tutta la loro sventura era originata dalla loro povertà. Il suo discorso presupponeva ch'ella si vendesse e ch'era spinta a farlo dalla povertà della sua famiglia. Ma essa non se ne accorse e le sue parole le sembrava una carezza eppoi pareva egli volesse biasimare solo se stesso.

In una società differente egli avrebbe potuto farla sua, pubblicamente, subito, senza imporle prima di darsi al sarto. Faceva proprie anche le menzogne di Angiolina, pur di renderla dolce e indurla a entrare in quelle idee, per sognare in due. Ella volle delle spiegazioni ed egli gliele diede beato di poter dar voce al sogno. Le raccontò quale lotta immane fosse scoppiata fra poveri e ricchi, i più e i meno. Non v'era da dubitare dell'esito della lotta il quale avrebbe apportato la libertà a tutti, anche a loro. Le parlò dell'annientamento del capitale e del mite breve lavoro che sarebbe stato l'obbligo d'ognuno. La donna uguale all'uomo e l'amore un dono reciproco (II, i, 540 –1).

[It was a dream which he continued to develop while with Angiolina, and regardless of her being there. He dreamed that they were very unhappy because of the unfair conditions of society under which they lived. He was so persuaded of this that he even imagined himself capable of performing an act of heroism in order to ensure the triumph of socialism. All their misfortunes were due to their poverty. His argument was based on the assumption that she was selling herself and that it was the poverty of her family which drove her to do so. But she did not perceive this implication and only regarded his words as a caress, and thought that he was blaming himself.

In another order of society he would at once have acknowledged her publicly without obliging her first to sacrifice herself to the tailor. He entered into Angiolina's lies in order to make her kinder to him and induce her to join in his ideas so that they might both dream together. She asked for some explanations and he gave them to her, only too glad to be able to utter his dream aloud. He told her of the enormous struggle which had broken out between rich and poor, great and small. There could be no doubt as to the issue of the struggle which was to bring liberty to all, to them as well. He talked to her about the abolition of capital and the short hours of agreeable work which alone one would be obliged to do. Woman was to be the equal of man and love a reciprocal gift.]

The use of 'sogno', 'sognare', 'menzogne', and above all the intellectual dishonesty which enables Brentani to act the rôle of a victim of circumstances, glossing over his personal failures, his absurd conviction that he could be a Socialist hero in some conveniently undefined way – everything reveals his dream for what it is. The final irony is the working-class girl's refusal to share it. The narrator's earlier statement that Brentani had indulged in Socialist ideas, of course without ever lifting a finger to realize them, is recalled at this point and helps to reveal the target of Svevo's irony, namely what Spriano, in a study of Socialism in Turin at this period,[2] has called 'il socialismo dei professori', the rather nebulous belief then current in intellectual and literary circles that an egalitarian society based on Marxist principles would somehow come about by a mysterious process of evolution.

If neither revolution nor evolution will bring about the good society, what then will, in Svevo's view? The only clue provided in *Senilità* is the presence of Signora Chierici and the active compassion which enables her to transcend her personal grief. Her presence is one factor which makes the world of *Senilità* less bleak than that of *Una vita*. It is not a comic novel, although it is enlivened from time to time by touches of humour – Angiolina's vulgarity, Balli's wit and even at times Brentani's – but a corrosive irony is ever present, and if we smile it is with tight lips, and more frequently *at* the characters than *with* them. The factor which most significantly distinguishes this novel from its predecessor on the thematic level is that its incorrigibly optimistic protagonist survives, and with less bitterness in his soul than he had when the novel opened. Imagery is indeed a disease, but 'health' is not all it seems to be, while he who dreams and runs away, lives to dream again another day.

5. The Years of Silence, 1898–1923

Svevo was bitterly disappointed at the reception the critics gave to *Senilità*. In six months it was reviewed six times. Silvio Benco's review in *L'Indipendente* (12 October 1898) was favourable, although he criticized Svevo's style and professed himself unable to understand the significance of the title. His fellow Triestine, Ida Finzi, writing in the Genoese *Supplemento al Caffaro* (11 February 1899) under the name of 'Haydée', praised Svevo's capacity for analysis. The other reviews were unfavourable, and the German novelist Paul Heyse, to whom Svevo had sent a copy of *Senilità*, wrote expressing regret that an author so gifted should waste his time on such an unworthy subject. The novel sold badly, and as late as 1925 Svevo was able to acquire twenty copies of the first edition. Unable to understand the general misunderstanding and indifference, he decided to give up writing. In the preface to the second edition of *Senilità*, written in March 1927, he wrote: 'Mi rassegnai al giudizio tanto unanime (non esiste una unanimità più perfetta del silenzio), e per venticinque anni m'astenni dallo scrivere' (II, i, *429*). [I resigned myself to this remarkably unanimous verdict – there is no form of unanimity more complete than silence – and for twenty-five years I abstained from writing.] He could not forget his disappointment: in 1903 his wife asked him to burn her letters to prevent their ever being read by anyone else, to which he replied that she need not worry. 'Io che ho pubblicato romanzi so che gli *altri* sono molto discreti' (I, *343*). [I, who have published two novels, know that *other people* are very discreet.] Later still he claimed to have given up literature completely, reading as well as writing. He wrote to Montale in 1926: 'Sento il bisogno di dirle che non credo che la differenze fra la *Coscienza* e i due romanzi precedenti debba ricercarsi nell'influenza di letteratura modernissima. Io ero molto ignorante quando scrissi perché dopo l'insuccesso di *Senilità* io proprio m'interdissi la letteratura' (I, *779*). [I think I ought to tell you I don't believe the difference between *La Coscienza* and the preceding two novels is to be attributed to the influence of very recent literature. I was very ignorant when I wrote it, because after the failure of *Senilità* I banned literature from my life.] And he stated in

1902 : 'Io, a quest'ora e definitivamente ho eliminato dalla mia vita quella ridicola e dannosa cosa che si chiama letteratura' (III, *818*). [Now and definitively, I have eliminated that ridiculous and harmful thing called literature from my life.]

This 'renunciation' was eventually rationalized, and Svevo decided that pressure of work and a sense of responsibility had prevented him from writing.

> Io mi ricordo che ... amai sempre il mio demone letterario. Non lo respinsi già per il dispiacere che non mi si volesse concedere la fama: temevo che m'impedisse di fare il dovere che m'ero imposto a vantaggio mio, dei miei, e anche dei miei soci. Era una questione d'onestà, perché poco ci voleva ad accorgersi che se scrivevo o leggevo una sola linea il mio lavoro era rovinato per una intera settimana (*Vita di mio marito*, p. 80). [I remember ... I always loved my literary demon. I did not repel him out of pique at being denied fame. I was afraid he might prevent me from discharging the obligations I had assumed on behalf of myself, my family, and my partners. It was a question of honesty, because it was obvious that if I wrote or read a single line, my work was ruined for a whole week.]

Svevo had for some time been hoping to be given a post in his father-in-law's paint-manufacturing firm. He had indeed almost given up hope, writing to his wife in 1898: 'Capisco che da quella parte come diciamo noi ebrei non viene il Messia' (I, *115*). [I realize, as we Jews say, the Messiah won't come from that direction.] In the following year, however, his imperious mother-in-law ordered him to resign from the bank and join the family business, for which he worked for the rest of his life. The years which followed were very active. He was regularly required to visit the Murano factory, as well as London, in addition to visits to France and Germany. Yet his account of these years, which is faithfully echoed by his wife's biography, contains several inconsistencies and leaves at least one mystery unexplained. Even before the serial publication of *Senilità* – 15 June to 16 September 1898 – he wrote to his wife on 26 May: 'Assisto proprio alla fine dei miei sogni estetici e questo quando ci penso trovo che sia molto male. Forse se arrivo alla vecchiaia avrò tempo di pentirmene sentendo di avere offeso la mia intima natura mancando al compito a cui per 38 anni mi credetti nato' (I, *115*). [This is really the end of my aesthetic dreams, and when I think about it, it seems a disaster. Perhaps, if I reach old age, I shall have time for regrets, since I feel I have offended against my inner nature by giving up the task which for 38 years I thought I was born for.] This outburst seems to have been provoked by the failure of a plan to leave the bank and set up in business with Adolfo. 'Renunciation' was evidently in his mind even before *Senilità* was published. Could it be that he had unconsciously anticipated its reception and was preparing himself for it?

And what did he in fact renounce? He certainly dedicated more time than before to his violin, but there was a standard of performance with that instrument beyond which he was unable to progress: those who knew him say that he played 'scolasticamente', and it is very doubtful whether music could ever have provided him with the particular emotional and intellectual satisfaction he derived from writing. At all events, he never ceased to *write*; it was publication he gave up. One of the recurrent themes of his correspondence in these years is the need to write. 'Deve esserci nel mio cervello qualche ruota che non sa cessare di fare quei romanzi che nessuno volle leggere ...' (I, *196*) [There must be in my brain some wheel that cannot stop creating those novels no-one wanted to read] he comments, after describing an absurd scheme for establishing a commercial empire, and Jonard has commented perceptively that even in his letters to his wife Svevo 'faisait de la littérature'. Publication, on the other hand, especially after the experience of *Senilità*, was another matter. 'Scrivere a questo mondo bisogna, ma pubblicare non occorre' (*Vita di mio marito*, p. 48). [One must write in this world, but there's no need to publish.] But perhaps when Svevo talked of eliminating 'literature' from his life the incorrigible ironist was talking of the 'manufactured product', the published book. Nor did he seem to be convinced by his own explanations if he wrote in 1906: 'Rietti mi disse che il fatto che io sono caduto fuori della letteratura non è la consequenza delle mie occupazioni ma della mia poltroneria. Tanto meglio che lo so, ma non mi serve a niente' (1, *44*). [Rietti told me that I had dropped out of literature on account of my indolence, not my business. All the better to know it, but it does no good.]

Svevo turned at this time to the theatre, his first love, perhaps in order to avoid further disappointment as a novelist. In October 1899 he was planning a play entitled *Degenerazione* which was never written, and in 1903 he was at work on *Un marito*, having already written *L'avventura di Maria*, but inevitably he soon returned to prose fiction.

Three tales with a Venetian setting belong to the period between 1900 and the First World War. They are *Marianno*, *Cimutti* and *In*

Serenella. The first describes the life of a boy from an orphanage who is given a home by a cooper who has no son and needs a cheap apprentice; the boy's tears and his lie that he had been given a gold medal which would enable his mother to recognize him verge on a Dickensian sentimentality only redeemed by the narrator's irony. Cimutti is a character-sketch of a warehouse foreman in Murano, and is based on a Veneziani employee. The principal interest of this tale, and of *In Serenella*, lies in the account they give of Svevo's detached view of himself as a manager. The kindly Signor Giulio, a 'sognatore' whose dreams make life more agreeable and who is sorry to see women dismissed because he knows how important their wages are to them, closely resembles Svevo; the dynamic brothers in Trieste are a thinly veiled but fundamentally affectionate caricature of Olga Veneziani. Signor Giulio's most absorbing occupation is to watch the effect of the changing light over the Serenella lagoon – eloquent testimony to Svevo's lack of interest in business, as well as to his perceptiveness and the influence of the visual arts on his work. Another story which belongs to this period is *Giacomo*, an account of conversations with a peasant whom the narrator meets while walking near Udine. Giacomo is an expert on work, which he dislikes intensely, and of the way in which it is done; his presence brings work to a halt and his finest achievement is to force his 'employers' to pay him to go away. These tales shed an interesting light on Svevo as a rather paternalistic employer who genuinely enjoyed chatting with workmen and peasants and as a writer who loved the Venetian dialect, which he often uses in direct speech.

Orazio Cima is a tale which has a Triestine setting, and contains important indications of Svevo's future development. Probably written during the First World War, *Orazio Cima* is set in 1886, when both Svevo and his first person singular narrator were twenty-five years old. Cima is a wealthy Abruzzese who has settled in Trieste and devotes himself to hunting; he also has a delightful mistress, Antonia. His character may owe something to that of the huntsman Ulfheim in Ibsen's *When We Dead Awaken* (1899). The narrator attaches himself to Cima because he finds him repellent; he is a strong, healthy extrovert, which the narrator is not, and his friendship is to be a 'cure'. Jonard assumes that things will end badly for the narrator, for is he not a weakling, doomed to lose in the struggle for life? The tale is unfinished, and so we cannot tell with certainty how it was to have ended; but why does the narrator, telling his story *post eventum*, insist that he had not realized how much he had desired Antonia? And why does he refer to his friend as 'poor Orazio'? A prototype of Zeno Cosini seems to be making a first appearance here, and characteristically feeling guilty at the improbable success he has experienced. A prototype of Zeno is certainly present in *Vino generoso*, a story written before the war and revised afterwards.

One characteristic which several of these stories have in common is that they are unfinished. Svevo was in the habit of writing in order to fix impressions and ideas before they faded in his memory, to which one could add that where there is no intention to publish there is no overwhelming need to put into a final form. Alternatively one could suggest that these tales were abandoned because Svevo felt an urgent need to finish other works – not only *La coscienza di Zeno*, but also such stories as *La novella del buon vecchio e della bella fanciulla*, the idea for which he had, according to his wife, discussed with James Joyce before the 1914–18 war and to which he returned in 1926.

It is unfortunate that Svevo's intellectual and cultural development during this period is badly documented. His library was destroyed during the 1939–45 war, so that we have only occasional hints of what he was reading. His *Epistolario* contains many letters from 1900–1914, to which we shall return later, but they are mostly to his wife and contain only occasional scraps of information of the kind one would like. For the vital period 1915–23, when he travelled little, we have only twenty-three letters. Even so, following indications given by Svevo in the *Profilo autobiografico*, it is possible to pick out two encounters which were to have a decisive influence on him; the first of these was his friendship with James Joyce, the second his reading of Freud.

In March 1905 Joyce took up a post as teacher of English at the Berlitz School in Trieste; two years later, after a few unsatisfactory months in Rome, he returned to Trieste as a freelance teacher giving private lessons. Svevo, whose spoken English was poor, became one of his pupils in 1907. Joyce was not a good teacher, but he was good for Svevo's morale. Joyce characteristically used his own poems and stories as a basis for his conversation classes; Svevo was very impressed by what he read, and in return gave Joyce copies of *Una vita* and *Senilità*, whereupon his teacher decided that Svevo was a neglected talent, the only contemporary Italian novelist worthy of interest he had so far discovered. As Furbank has observed, both men benefited from the friendship. There is little tangible evidence of Joyce's influence on Svevo's writing, but the renewed confidence his encouragement gave him in his ability as a writer was of inestimable importance.

The Years of Silence

Joyce's enthusiasm never waned during Svevo's lifetime, and it was he who was largely responsible for the warm reception given to *La coscienza* in Parisian literary circles, while the lecture which Svevo gave on Joyce in Milan in 1927 reveals the Triestine's lasting gratitude for the generosity with which the Irishman had espoused his cause.

The extent of Freud's influence on Svevo is difficult to estimate if only because Svevo, as always, tried to minimize its importance, and his statements on the subject do not always clarify matters. We cannot say, for example, which of Freud's works he read, or precisely when: 'Lessi dei libri di Freud nel 1908 se non sbaglio' (III, 685) [I read some of Freud's books in 1908, if I am not mistaken], is Svevo's memory, perhaps deliberately kept vague. On the other hand, his knowledge of Freud was not necessarily limited to those of Freud's works which he was able to read. Trieste was Austrian, and whereas in Italy both Crocean idealism and orthodox Roman Catholicism strongly opposed the spread of Freudianism, the Austrian city, and particularly its Jewish community, was relatively free of these influences and more inclined towards the positivist tradition in which Freud's ideas were rooted. Viennese literary and scientific journals circulated in the city, and Freud's theories were the subject of discussions which are well chronicled in R. Ellmann's detailed biography of Joyce – discussions between Joyce, Svevo and Edoardo Weiss, a practising psychoanalyst who corresponded with Freud and later applied Freudian theories to the criticism of Manzoni and *I promessi sposi*.

Freudianism was always presented to Svevo in an ambiguous light. Its scientific methods belonged to the tradition of positivistic rationalism which went back to the Enlightenment and in which Svevo had been brought up, and on the other hand Freud himself had indicated similarities between his thought and that of Schopenhauer which appealed to Thomas Mann and were bound also to appeal to Svevo. Above all, Freudianism codified and gave scientific form to Svevo's own perceptions, offering him a conceptual framework in terms of which he could express his vision of the human mind and develop his themes of 'sickness' and 'health'. At the same time there were always sceptical voices – not those of the Croceans or the Catholics, but of sceptics like Joyce, who told Svevo he preferred confession and St Thomas Aquinas. And Svevo himself in 1910 saw the failure of a relative, Bruno Veneziani, to achieve a cure through psychoanalysis in Vienna:

> ... la psicanalisi? Io la conobbi nel 1910. Un mio amico nevrotico (referred to elsewhere as 'un congiunto') corse a Vienna per

intraprenderla. L'avviso dato a me fu l'unico buon effetto della sua cura. Si fece psicanalizzare per due anni e ritornò dalla cura addirittura distrutto: abulico come prima ma con la sua abulia aggravata dalla convinzione ch'egli, essendo fatto cosi, non potesse agire altrimenti. È lui che mi diede la convinzione che fosse pericoloso di spiegare ad un uomo com'era fatto ... (III, 688) [Psychoanalysis? I came across it in 1910. A neurotic friend of mine ... dashed to Vienna to take it up. That I was told about it was the only good that came of his course of treatment. He had himself analysed for two years and came back from the course positively shattered: lacking in will-power as before, but with his aboulia aggravated by the conviction that since that was his nature he could not behave differently. It was he who convinced me that it was dangerous to explain a man's nature to him.]

It is possible to outline the probable course of Svevo's interest in Freud as follows. First came an initial interest, even enthusiasm, with the discussions and reading in the years 1908–10. There is uncertainty as to what exactly he did read, but it is impossible to believe that at this stage he read no Freud at all: when he was interested in Darwinism he had gone back to the source and read Darwin rather than his popularizers. Doubts aroused in the discussions would have been made stronger in 1910. In 1918 he gained a closer and more expert knowledge of one aspect of Freud's work when he helped Aurelio Finzi, his nephew and also a doctor, to translate 'l'opera del Freud "sul sogno"' [Freud's work 'on dreams'] (*Vita di mio marito*, p. 94), by which is probably meant the brief *On Dreams* (1901). At about the same time his curiosity led him, in complete contradiction to Freudian theory, to experiment with autoanalysis.

Svevo remained unable to dispel his doubts about the therapeutic value of Freudianism, but as he wrote in 1926, 'quale scrittore potrebbe rinunziare di pensar almeno la psicanalisi?' (III, 688) [what writer could refrain from thinking at least in terms of psychoanalysis?] He accepted the model of the mind which it postulated and, moreover, he was attracted by the possibilities for irony which it revealed, not merely in terms of the 'Freudian slip' (such as the episode of Guido Speier's funeral in *La coscienza di Zeno*, in which Zeno follows the wrong hearse), but in more general terms too, which suggest that daily life may be fraught with hidden tensions and inner conflicts. There was no great inconsistency in Svevo's attitude towards the new science, since Freud wrote in the 1926 edition of the *Encyclopaedia Britannica* that the term *psychoanalysis* had by now 'come

The Years of Silence

to have two meanings : (1) a particular method of treating nervous disorders and (2) the science of unconscious mental processes, which has also been appropriately described as "depth psychology"'. It would also have been clear to Svevo that not everyone who accepted Freud's findings under the second heading necessarily shared his views concerning the first. Svevo's attitude was very like that of Joyce and Kafka among contemporary novelists, and that of many psychologists today.

In 1919, in what he called 'un attimo di forte travolgente ispirazione' [a moment of strong, overwhelming inspiration], he began *La coscienza di Zeno*, which was the first novel to make extensive use of Freudian theory. Naturally – and justifiably – proud of his achievement, Svevo in 1923 showed the novel to Edoardo Weiss, hoping that he would review it in a professional journal. Svevo's subsequent account, in the *Soggiorno londinese* of 1928 and his letters of 1927-28 to Valerio Jahier, make it clear that he was deeply hurt by Weiss's observation that his novel revealed only ignorance of psychoanalysis. One of his aims in that essay and his letters, serious for all their bantering tone, is to minimize the extent of his indebtedness to Freud and at the same time to argue that any possible misunderstanding on his part did not *ipso facto* invalidate the novel as a work of art. Freudianism, in the person of Weiss, has rejected Svevo; Svevo will now, as far as he can, reject Freudianism. Since he is on the defensive he naturally expresses himself in terms of self-deprecating irony and the remarks in the *Soggiorno londinese* are not to be taken at their face value. The wounded tone of these writings also prompts the reflection that they come from the pen of the frustrated and disappointed Ettore Schmitz, rather than from that of the urbane and detached Italo Svevo, Schmitz's 'second self'.

The influence of Freud and Joyce, however, is not enough by itself to explain why Svevo should have felt compelled to work with such urgency on his new novel in 1919 rather than at any point in the previous few years. Svevo rarely committed himself to any clear and unambiguous statements about his work, but in suggesting that Freudianism was not an overwhelmingly important source of inspiration for him, is it not possible that he was indicating, in customarily oblique fashion, that there had been another important stimulus? The 1914-18 war was such a stimulus. Perhaps it was the need to write about the war – or, more precisely, to set his narrative against a background of war – that led him to abandon the earlier, unfinished, tales and turn instead to works in which an awareness of the war setting is essential to an understanding of their themes, or which have as their background the post-war return to 'normality'.

The outbreak of war, which had been expected for so long that hostilities took most people by surprise, saw Svevo working for the Veneziani firm. The collapse of the Second International in 1914 and the failure of the Socialists to stop the war probably came as a disappointment to him. In 1915 he had to go to Germany to supervise the manufacture there of the 'Moravian Anti-Fouling composition' which he and his associates were now selling to the navies of all the principal belligerents in the war. A Socialist with pacifist leanings making a profit out of the war! The situation was not of his making or desiring, but it nevertheless inspired guilt feelings in Svevo which he was later to externalize in *La coscienza*.

What Svevo saw of the war preparations in Germany convinced him that Germany would win. He had no admiration for German militarism, but he was impressed by the patriotism of the Germans and the way in which science was being harnessed to aid the military. He also thought the war would be short, as did many people at the time. We know now that he was wrong on both counts. The long and bloody conflict came to an apparently sudden end in 1918, bringing about, paradoxically, the realization of one of his dreams, the unification of Trieste with Italy.

Conversations with members of Svevo's family give the impression that he had always had vaguely pacifist leanings but that it was not until the horrors of modern warfare had outraged his humanitarian feelings that he took an active interest in the political problems of preserving the peace; it was probably at this time that he studied the pacifist writings of Alfred Fried (1864–1921) and Walter Schücking (1875–1935), under whose influence he began to write a treatise *Sulla teoria della pace*, only fragments of a draft of which survive. Whether or not it was ever completed we shall never know; the *Profilo autobiografico* implies that it was.

The *Pace e guerra* section was written during the war. The *Teoria della pace* section was written in 1919, when the growing public demand that some steps be taken to prevent the renewal of the suffering and destruction involved in modern warfare was leading towards the formulation of proposals to found the League of Nations. Italy's decision to join the League may have made the completion and publication of the *Teoria della pace* unnecessary, but even in its fragmentary state the treatise is moving in its humanitarian rejection of war and of the jingoistic patriotism which that war in particular provoked: 'La guerra è e resta una cosa turpe per ogni uomo equilibrato e morale. La sua turpitudine non è diminuita né dal patriottismo né dall'eroismo' (III, 661). [War is and remains vile for every balanced, moral man. Its vileness is not diminished either by patriotism or heroism.] And it is at times a strange document, especially when Svevo puts forward rivalry in trade as the alternative to war and writes of the civilizing benefits of the free passage across national frontiers of goods, men and ideas; one feels one might be reading one of those innumerable treatises on commerce produced during the Enlightenment. Indeed, only through Enlightened Despotism on an international scale could Svevo's theories be put into practice.

Ultimately, however, Svevo's response to the war was bound to be that of the creative artist rather than that of the political theorist. His return to narrative fiction was inevitable, in the circumstances, and if the war played as important a part in inspiring *La coscienza*, as I think it did, then that fact will in turn influence our interpretation of the novel.

The apparent suddenness with which the war came to an end probably surprised Svevo, as it did many others. It brought rejoicing at the reuniting of his family, at unification with Italy – and a euphoria which is reflected in the light tone of the articles he wrote in 1919 for *La nazione* (III, 624–30). At the same time there is a sceptical note about certain passages of *Sulla teoria della pace*, as though the author did not believe that his ideal could be realized. And what about that other ideal, the Socialist future? Had 1917 not brought its realization nearer?

There is no direct comment in Svevo's work on the Russian revolution, but one passage in the tale *Vino generoso*, of uncertain date, is very revealing. The elderly narrator's illness and stringent diet have made him forget his 'scientific socialism'.

> Spaventato e immiserito, avevo lasciato morire qualunque mio istinto generoso per far posto a pastiglie, gocce e polverette. Non più socialismo. Che cosa poteva importarmi se la terra, contrariamente ad ogni più illuminata conclusione scientifica, continuava ad essere l'oggetto di proprietà privata? Se a tanti, perciò, non era concesso il pane quotidiano e quella parte di libertà che dovrebbe adornare ogni giornata dell'uomo? Avevo io forse l'uno o l'altro? (III, 65). [Frightened and depressed, I had let all my generous instincts die to make room for pastilles, drops and powders. No more socialism. What could it matter to me that the land, contrary to all the most enlightened scientific ideas,

was still private property? What if on that account many people did not get their daily bread and the modicum of liberty that should adorn every day of a man's life? Had I either the one or the other?]

The illogicality and the egoism of the argument are obvious, although the author, in a story which is moving towards the technique of *La coscienza*, does not intervene to point them out. The narrator then quarrels with his nephew Giovanni, who is an unashamed capitalist, over the 'struggle for money', losing his temper and shouting: 'Ti appenderemo ... Non meriti altro. La corda al collo e dei pesi alle gambe.' Giovanni replies: 'Già, tutti i socialisti finiscono in practica col ricorrere al mestiere del carnefice' (III, 66). ['We will hang you ... You don't deserve anything else. A rope round your neck and weights on your feet.' 'Yes, in practice all socialists end up calling in the executioner.'] On one level this is a facile polemic, the bourgeois inveighing against the murderous Bolsheviks. But on another level it encapsulates a truth which Svevo found unpalatable: that the Socialist version of the good society was based on the premise of a revolution which, if historical precedents and the death of the Russian Imperial family in 1918 were any guide, was to cost many their lives. How could one reconcile this willingness to kill with love of humanity? Svevo could not, for he believed that the impulse towards conflict was too strong to be denied: mankind's one faint hope lay in channelling it into other directions as described in *Sulla teoria della pace*.

6. *La coscienza di Zeno*, 1923

La conscienza di Zeno seems to have gone through three stages before publication in 1923. First there was the original draft which Svevo wrote under the pressure of an urgent sense of inspiration in 1919. Then came the revised and polished version on which he worked for the next three years and which formed the basis of the typescript he sent to the publisher Cappelli in 1922. This version was apparently too long and several cuts were made in it, giving a final version which was rather shorter than Svevo had intended. The first two versions have not survived and the third exists only in book form, so that we are unable to analyse the changes which Svevo made between 1919 and 1923.

To readers of Svevo's previous novels and stories much in *La coscienza* will seem familiar and much new and original. The narrator-protagonist, Zeno Cosini, has a familiar air; he was described by Svevo as an older and wealthier brother of Nitti and Brentani, and like them he is weak-willed and given to introspection and self-deception. Like the protagonists of *Orazio Cima* and *Vino generoso*, he tells his own story in the first person singular, and so convincingly are his character and his view of events presented that the novel is a remarkable *tour de force* of technique. Some readers have seen the use of a first person singular narrator as a simplification, a means of pushing the novel in the direction of autobiography – a view which rests on the assumption, which will be considered later, that Svevo can be identified with Zeno. Others have seen it as a negative achievement, a solution to the problem of how to get rid of the obtrusive author. This is true in the sense that the technique obviates the need for auctorial comment, but it is a view which fails to take account of the positive aspect of Svevo's achievement, namely that he is able to create an intense illusion of reality when dealing with Zeno's moral and psychological problems. One may laugh with Zeno or at him; one may be charmed by his irrepressible optimism or appalled by his egoism; one may, indeed, be charmed and appalled at the same time' and so be disturbed and challenged by the ambivalence of one's reactions, as was probably Svevo's intention, but it is in any case impossible to remain indifferent or deny Zeno's reality.

The novel's title carries several meanings. It refers to Zeno's conscience, that disturbing voice which constantly adduces his apparently successful survival as evidence of guilt. It refers also to Zeno's conscious mind, as opposed to his unconscious; and it may also refer to different levels of awareness in the two Zenos – one the narrator, the other a character in a story of his own creating. For *La coscienza* is the first novel to make extensive use of Freudian theory and to base its structure on psychoanalysis. This is the source of much that is new in the work – Zeno's obsessive preoccupation with numbers and dates, for example. Boswell wrote that 'One has a strange propensity to fix some point of time from when a better course of life may begin'. The points of time which Zeno fixes for such amendments of life fill his diaries and so cover the walls of his room when he is a student that on changing lodgings he has to have them redecorated. Many of the dates refer to unfulfilled resolutions to give up smoking, and Svevo's awareness of the importance of compulsive habits is another debt to Freud.

It is, however, Svevo's brilliant handling of psychosomatic illness which owes most to Freud. Zeno is a hypochondriac in search of a disease which will impose shape and discipline on his life. When, towards the end of the novel, his doctor tentatively, but wrongly, diagnoses diabetes, Zeno studies the disease and is delighted by the regular habits which it imposes on those who suffer from it. But throughout the novel Zeno suffers from a variety of aches and pains which have their origin in the defeats and humiliations which he endures. He is initially convinced that he is ill: 'La malattia, è una convinzione ed io nacqui con quella convinzione' (II, ii, 607). [Ill-health is a conviction, and I was born with that conviction.] His 'malattia "dolente"' (II, ii, 680), on the other hand, has a specific origin, narrated in the account of his encounter with the crippled Tullio, who suffers from rheumatism. He has studied anatomy, and tells Zeno that one has to move no less than fifty-four muscles in half a second in order to walk. Awareness of this fact makes Zeno limp, and his subsequent meeting with Ada, the girl he wishes to marry, and Guido Speier, his rival, makes his limp worse. Later that evening, as a result of his humiliation at Guido's hands, he experiences for the first time the 'stabbing pain' which never leaves him for long and which he regards as 'lo stigma del vinto' (II, ii, 711) [brand of defeat].

Other characters in the novel suffer from illnesses which have a recognizable physical cause. Ada is transformed by Basedow's disease (exophthalmic goitre) into a grotesque caricature of her formerly beautiful self. Her father, Giovanni Malfenti, and Zeno's friend Copler are also seriously ill, and Zeno at one point engages with them in a curious discussion about 'real' and 'imaginary' illnesses, in which the sick men state the merits of afflictions for which some specific treatment can be prescribed, whereas for Zeno's 'imaginary' illness there is no cure. But when he writes this account, Zeno is alive and apparently well: Malfenti and Copler are both dead. Where, then lies true health? Running through the novel is the theme that health and illness, like true wits to madness, are 'near allied', and 'thin partitions do their bounds divide'. One has the habit of changing into the other when the reader least expects it.

La coscienza di Zeno is a comic masterpiece, and the comedy will seem new to readers of Svevo's bleaker earlier novels. Zeno's humour and cheerfulness may pose problems of interpretation, but the element of comedy need not surprise us; Svevo's wit was a constant source of pleasure to his friends. Several of his earlier plays are comedies, and many of his letters to his wife are delightful pieces of humorous writing. He is witty at his own expense in the *Diario per la fidanzata* and other diary fragments, and although he may have known *Jokes and their Relation to the Unconscious* (1905) he did not need Freud to teach him that humour could be a defence-mechanism.

We learn from the very first page of the novel that Zeno is a man of means who, because he is suffering from certain personality problems, has himself psychoanalysed in the hope of finding a cure to his various ailments. His course of analysis takes place from late 1914 to April 1915, but he first approaches the analyst, known only as Dr S., early in 1914 at what turns out to be an awkward moment since the latter is about to leave Trieste for a lengthy period of time. Anxious to progress quickly, Dr S. invites his elderly patient to write about himself, beginning with his addiction to smoking. The novel then takes the form of Zeno's memoirs, published by the analyst out of pique when his patient refuses to continue with his course of treatment. This simple expedient is basically an up-to-date variant of one of the oldest devices in the history of novel-writing, the convention whereby the author presents himself or one of his characters to the public in the guise of an editor of documents which circumstances have brought into his possession. But in this context it has far-reaching implications for the construction and the consequent interpretation of the novel.

Dr S., in his *Prefazione*, admits that his method was unorthodox:

'Debbo scusarmi di aver indotto il mio paziente a scrivere la sua autobiografia; gli studiosi di psicoanalisi arricceranno il naso a tanta novità' (II, ii, 599). [I must apologize for having persuaded my patient to write his autobiography. Students of psychoanalysis will turn their noses up at such an unorthodox proceeding.] Freud in fact repeatedly warned that 'It is wrong to set a patient tasks, such as collecting his memories or thinking over some particular period in his life' since he has to learn to avoid 'all criticism of the unconscious and its derivatives'. He thought observation of this rule particularly necessary with patients 'who practise the art of sheering off into intellectual discussion during their treatment, who speculate a great deal and often very wisely about their condition and in that way avoid doing anything to overcome it'[1] – patients such as Zeno in fact.

The reason for this advice is simple. Freudian analysis depends very largely upon a process of free association; a deliberate and systematic process of recalling, on the other hand, allows the censorship mechanism to come into play. As Zeno says, 'Una confessione in iscritto è sempre menzognera' (II, ii, 928) [A written confession is always mendacious] – but for psychological reasons, not for the linguistic reasons which he misleadingly adduces. And what a splendid sense of timing makes Svevo attribute these words to him just as Zeno is about to put on paper (and in what he hopes will pass for Tuscan) the 'truth' about the lies he now claims to have told his analyst. This is a factor of which Zeno himself would have been aware, since he has read a book on psychoanalysis in order to 'assist' his analyst. Zeno's only attempt to practise the free-association method is described in the *Preambolo*, which we are to believe is the first part of the novel written by Zeno, and it is very revealing; the disturbing sounds made by his dying father's breathing are connected with the visual image of a railway train and dismissed as irrelevant. Its significance is revealed in the chapter dealing with the death of his father. All this is very Freudian and suggests that Svevo had read Freud more carefully than he was prepared to admit. At all events the doctor's preface, with its statement that Zeno's memoirs are a mixture of truth and falsehood, warns us that in Zeno we have to do with an unreliable narrator who, whether he knows it or not, is lying. One admires Svevo's skill: with remarkable economy he has put us on our guard against Zeno the deceiver and has done by implication what other novelists have found it necessary to do explicitly, namely to dissociate themselves from their first-person narrators.[2]

This puts the reader into a particularly dynamic relationship with the protagonist as Zeno tells his story. And at this point it is well to remind ourselves who Zeno's reader is. For if it is necessary to distinguish between Svevo and Zeno, the superior, clear-sighted ironist and his devious narrator, it is equally legitimate to distinguish between their readers. *We* are Svevo's readers; the novelist creates his characters, sets them in motion, and writes for whoever will read. Zeno the character, in the fiction which Svevo has devised, writes for another character who is equally Svevo's creation – the absent analyst, absent for we know not what reason for the first seven chapters, supposedly written by Zeno before analysis, and absent once more, this time in neutral Switzerland, when Zeno writes the final section (*Psico-analisi*). Physically absent, he is nevertheless felt as a 'presence' throughout the novel, since even before analysis Zeno writes as though on the defensive, as though attributing to Dr S. attitudes which are those of his disturbing conscience. Zeno continually feels the need, not to reveal himself and so progress towards a cure, but to defend himself. In effect there is a constant tension between the supposed writer of these memoirs and his fictional reader, Dr S., so that it comes as no surprise when Zeno rejects as unjust a diagnosis – that he is suffering from an Oedipus complex – which he regards as an accusation, and which he prefers to interpret as a manifestation of the analyst's personality problems: 'Chissà perché si sia preso di tale odio per me? Anche lui dev'essere un istericone che per aver desiderato invano sua madre se ne vendica su chi non c'entra affatto' (11,ii, *937*). [I wonder why he took such a violent dislike to me. He is probably also an hysteric, who avenges himself for having lusted after his mother, by tormenting innocent people.] He reacts in a similar way to Ada's accusation that he had never loved Guido, closing his eyes and covering his face. 'Poi nell'oscurità rividi il cadavere di Guido e nella sua faccia sempre stampato lo stupore di essere là, privato della vita. Spaventato, rizzai la testa. Era preferibile affrontare l'accusa di Ada che io sapevo ingiusta che guardare nell'oscurità' (11,ii, *923*). [Then in the darkness I saw again Guido's dead body, still wearing that expression of astonishment on his face at finding himself lying there lifeless. I raised my head in horror. It was better to face Ada's accusations, unjust as they were, than to go on looking into the dark.]

From time to time, of course, Zeno will speculate, as Freud knew such patients would, about the workings of his unconscious mind, as when he suggests that in blaming his ills on to his habit of smoking he was merely looking for a scapegoat. But on the whole, 'guardare nell'oscurità' in the sense of looking into the darker recesses of his mind is what he will not do. That is the function of his reader, the absent analyst. There are indications, however, that he is disqualified from doing so, and that this function has to be exercised by Svevo's reader.

Svevo's reader is warned by the very existence of the *Prefazione*, as well as by its contents, that Zeno is maladjusted, although in what respect and to what extent we have initially no way of telling. Dr S. also introduces us to the notion of transference, 'the process whereby a patient shifts affects applicable to another person on to the analyst'.[3] Zeno's antipathy towards Dr S., the latter implies, is a manifestation of the hostility he feels towards his father. Dr S. also unwittingly reveals that counter-transference has taken place, 'the transference by the analyst of his repressed feelings upon the analysand'. Dr S. is, moreover, unprofessional in publishing the memoirs, and possibly incompetent too, since he seems complacently to present his diagnosis to Zeno long before his patient is ready to receive it. Freud warned that '"wild" psychoanalysis', with 'lightning diagnoses and "express" treatments', would arouse opposition in the patient and deter him from treatment, and it is possible that Svevo derived his concept of Dr S.'s character and methods from Freud's warnings about what the analyst should not do. Not that Svevo is merely satirizing an incompetent individual; in the person of Dr S. he is calling into question the adequacy of psycho-therapy to deal with what Svevo regards, as we shall see later, as one of society's most urgent problems.

After such a preface we are on our guard. We refrain from identifying with Zeno, and we read his memoirs from a point of view akin to, but not identical with, that of the analyst – akin to the analyst's, in the sense that we attempt as far as we can to sort out the truth from the lies; not identical with his, in the sense that we do not and are surely not intended to feel for Zeno the antagonism which he has aroused in Dr S.: Svevo's ideal reader is a lucid, detached observer, and such a reader will, as the novel progresses, find himself in the position of knowing more about Zeno than Zeno does himself. He will reject as false many of the claims which Zeno makes and will observe the emergence in Zeno's narrative of certain recurrent behaviour-patterns.

Zeno's memoirs, chapters 2 to 8 of the novel, fall into two sections. Chapters 2 to 7 are written before analysis, chapter 8 after. There is no attempt to tell Zeno's life story in straightforward chronological sequence; instead, after his preamble, he arranges his material under key headings. This is a controlled process, the opposite both of

Freudian free association and the Joycean stream of consciousness. Thus chapter 3 describes his addiction to smoking and his attempts to give it up, and moves in time from early childhood to the present: chapter 4 deals with his relations with his father and the traumatic experience of the latter's death. This is a brief section and covers a short period of time. Chapters 5 and 6 relate his excursions into matrimony and adultery; these are longer chapters which cover an undefined period of time beginning after the death of his father, and overlapping with chapter 7, which deals with his business association with Guido Speier. Joyce, excessively concerned as usual with questions of technique, was greatly impressed by Svevo's treatment of time in *La coscienza di Zeno*. Svevo's method enables Zeno not only to range freely over the events of his life, looking at some periods from several different points of view, but also to look at the past in the light of the present. More importantly, however, Zeno's habit of dividing his life into self-contained segments enables him to give mutually incompatible accounts of himself which will deceive the unwary, while at the same time key ideas and behaviour-patterns gain strength and importance by dint of repetition and variation in different circumstances. Compulsive habits, obsessions and fetishes, introspection, doubt, humiliation and illness are all recurrent features of Zeno's life. His ability to see himself in retrospect as a comic character is the principal source of the novel's humour, which Zeno is using to conceal three truths: firstly, that hostility is the keynote of all his personal relationships save one; secondly, that he is a compulsive liar; and thirdly, that guilt feelings colour the account he gives of himself.

Let us consider the question of hostility first. Smoking is for Zeno more than a habit, more indeed than a useful scapegoat on which he can blame his shortcomings. The cigarette is a virility-symbol, and rivalry with his father, from whom he steals cigar-ends and money, is the keynote of 'Il fumo,' as it is of 'La morte di mio padre', and it is especially notable that in the latter section when Cosini *père* is fit and well his son feels weak and insignificant; when the father is ill or confused the positions are reversed. The death of his father then dominates the son's life. Zeno feels guilty for having wished his father dead and he feels resentment at his father's last acts – the blow he struck his son in the last moment of his life, and the posthumous blow whereby in his will he made his son his heir but prevented him from managing the family business, nominating Olivi as his administrator. Zeno is thus made to feel permanently inferior.

In Freudian psychology the death of the father leaves the son feeling exposed; a living father is, as it were, an insurance policy against one's own death, and the death of one's father, conversely, puts one next in line to die. Zeno, who is a hypochondriac, looks about for a father-figure to whom he can attach himself. Guido Speier is a rival and so not eligible, but as a rival he is treated with the same hostility. Olivi, too, is regarded with resentment. But it is Giovanni Malfenti, Zeno's father-in-law, who comes nearest to being his father-substitute. Zeno admires his 'quiet strength', does his best to imitate him and marries into his family, yet their relationship, especially during Malfenti's last illness, is based on hostility. At this point one suspects that the analyst's diagnosis of an Oedipus complex may be accurate as far as it goes, and transference is consistent with this recurrent pattern.

Yet what about the women in Zeno's life? He proposes to Ada, mainly because he wishes to come under the tutelage of her father, and he resents her initial failure to take him seriously. During the table-turning episode he returns her anger with fantasies in which she asks a forgiveness which he sternly refuses to grant. He takes a mistress, Carla, whom he regards as a threat to his domestic tranquillity, and to whose declaration that he is her first lover he replies that she is his first mistress since marriage to 'balance the accounts'. He frequently feels an anger towards her which he expresses 'urlando delle parole dolcissime' (II, ii, 772) [uttering the sweetest nothings at the top of my voice]. He repeatedly humiliates her and his own suggestion that Dr S. is 'anche lui ... un istericone che per aver desiderato invano sua madre se ne vendica su chi non c'entra affatto' (II, ii, 937) [also an hysteric, who avenges himself for having lusted after his mother, by tormenting innocent people] provokes the reaction that the statement could well be applied to him. May not that 'anche' be an interesting Freudian slip?

The one person who is not treated with hostility is Augusta. At first she is ignored by Zeno, who is neatly manœuvred into marrying her by his scheming mother-in-law's decision to bring matters to a head. Augusta loves him devotedly and uncritically; but she does more than that. She brings to his life a comfort, order and regularity which he has not known for many years. When he is ill in body or uneasy in mind she consoles and absolves him; or rather she offers him a consolation which he is quick to turn into the absolution of which he is really in need. Augusta takes over many of the functions of the mother whom Zeno remembers with an affection unsoiled by guilt. It is no coincidence that Augusta's smile reminds him of his mother's, for she is a mother-figure *par excellence*, aptly compared to the swallow which builds its nest as soon as she has found her mate. She mothers her husband as well as her child, and it was Zeno's need for such a wife that led him unconsciously to alienate the unsuitable Ada.

Zeno naturally gives a rather different account of these relationships from that offered in these pages since, as we were warned, his memoirs are a mixture of truth and lies. One could perhaps go as far as to say that for Zeno the word 'truth' has a meaning very different from that which it has for most people. This is far from being the only piece of semantic confusion in the work: 'last cigarette', 'last betrayal', 'last embrace', words like 'health' and 'disease', all change their meaning according to the demands of circumstances. A number of incidents illustrate Zeno's flexible concept of truth and serve both to season the novel with humour and also to reinforce the initial warning about his unreliability.

In order to engage the attention of the Malfenti sisters, for example, he relates incidents from his as yet unfinished student days. He has what he calls the 'malattia della parola' [word-sickness] (II, ii, 659) and cannot open his mouth without misrepresenting things or people, otherwise he would see no point in talking. The stories he tells the girls illustrate the point perfectly. He subsequently learns from Augusta that none of the sisters had believed his anecdotes at the time, and his comment that the serious Ada was the only one to be outraged by his lies confirms that their assessment was correct. For Zeno, however, the stories are true in the special sense that it would have been impossible for him to tell them differently; without any conscious effort on his part, or so he claims, they constantly underwent slight modifications to make them more interesting. Even this statement cannot be accepted unreservedly, but it strikes me as being as near to the truth as one can expect from Zeno, whose honesty is rather like that of young children, who describe things not as they are but as they would like them to be.

Naturally there are occasions when Zeno, who is making an effort to tell the truth, admits to having lied. When he meets Tullio, for example, he is in low spirits and needs someone to feel sorry for him. He therefore tells his friend that he is grossly overworked. 'Non sei mica da invidiare, tu!' reflects the cripple. 'La conclusione era esatta', is Zeno's precise comment (II, ii, 682) [I must say I don't envy you ... The conclusion was right]; that it was based on a false premise is, in his view, of no consequence. The same cheerful disregard for correct logical sequences is exemplified in his relations with his wife. It is enough for him to attribute his distress to 'enforced idleness' or the fear of old age for her to extend to him the soothing affection and compassion for which he craves. Response, not the means by which it is achieved, is the all-important consideration. It comes as no surprise, then, to realize that his frankness is often more apparent than real; if he admits on occasions to lying, it does not follow that on other occasions he is telling the truth. He may be lying or he may, more subtly, be telling just as much of the truth as is necessary in order to deceive. Nowhere can these tendencies be seen more clearly than in his account of his relationship with Carla and Guido.

Zeno has an admirable wife in Augusta but he also takes a mistress. His conscience requires that he justify his conduct, which he does by presenting his first meeting with Carla as the result of his philanthropy, brought about at Copler's, not his, initiative, and he repeats his visits to her with the excuse that he is furthering her musical education. The pose of educator and benefactor to the girls they seduce is one which Svevo's protagonists find particularly congenial. Telling Augusta that he has met the girl enables him to feel innocent in spite of the attraction which she is beginning to exert over him, but he is disingenuous when, in answer to his wife's query about Carla's looks, he replies only that she seems rather anaemic. Only Zeno could be satisfied with the logic of his claim that 'Fino ad allora non avevo da rimproverarmi altro che di aver taciuto con Augusta. Ecco che ora ero innocente del tutto' (II,ii, 745). [Up to now I had nothing to reproach myself with, except having hidden it from Augusta. So that now I was completely innocent.] This incomplete account has satisfactory results since it forestalls any suspicions on the part of both Augusta and Copler while at the same time making Zeno more affectionate towards his wife. His walk to the park is a partial yielding to temptation, and he tells Augusta, wrongly, that he has been going there for some time to read his newspaper. When his unquestioning wife accepts this explanation, Zeno immediately converts it into permission to follow his inclination. It is true that the next day prudence, which he describes as virtue, reasserts itself and he walks in the opposite direction, but the chance discovery of a book on singing converts this inclination into a duty. From that point on his adultery is characterized by its high moral tone. The reader's mind goes back to Zeno's earlier remarks that when he wanted to revisit Carla, 'I pretesti...non mi sarebbero mica mancati' (II,ii, 745). [I might easily have found an excuse.] So does Zeno's, for his conclusion is 'Avevo trovato qualche cosa di più di un pretesto per poter fare quello ch'era il mio desiderio' (II, ii, *748*). [I had found something better than an excuse for doing what I wanted to do.]

What is surprising, after this, is Zeno's claim to have sacrificed Carla to Augusta. In so far as Carla renounced him he was at that point a victim of circumstances, but in retrospect he casts himself in an active, not a passive, rôle. Yet where he had in reality taken the initiative, he now casts himself in a passive rôle and presents himself as the victim of circumstances. He claims that it was music that led him back to Carla, that Augusta herself precipitated matters, and that he has in retrospect the feeling that he committed adultery because he was dragged into it. Zeno, like other characters, is a determinist when it suits him to be.

Zeno's account of his relations with Guido is equally implausible. That he envies Guido at their first meeting, and continues to do so, is clear. His contempt for Guido's taste, as characterized by his ivory-handled walking-stick and his rather vulgar bowing in the performance of the Bach chaconne, were no doubt real at the time, but hindsight has surely intensified the virulence of the 'imbecille' (II, ii, *694*) and the 'ciarlatano' (II, ii, *701*) which Zeno hurls at his memory. Here more than ever one is aware of the inextricable confusion of past and present in Zeno's mind.

Towards the end of Zeno's affair with Carla there is an episode which is very instructive. They meet Tullio by chance in the park. Carla is introduced as a friend of Augusta, to which Zeno adds the second lie that she, like Tullio, had sat down beside him without seeing him, as Tullio had. This unnecessary lie leads Tullio to conclude that Carla is Zeno's mistress. 'Il mentitore dovrebbe tener presente che per essere creduto non bisogna dire che le menzogne necessarie' (II, ii, *803*). [It is important to remember, if one is going to tell lies, that one must tell only essential ones if one wants to be believed.] This dictum of Zeno's can usefully be applied to himself in other circumstances, coming as it does shortly before the story of his partnership with Guido. Zeno explains too much when accounting for his eagerness to work with his brother-in-law, and some of his statements are implausible. One is never convinced, for example, by his insistent complaints about his enforced idleness, since the terms of his father's will excluded him from the management of his own affairs but could not prevent him from working. The pose, however, is one he finds congenial. He also maintains that he wished to become a businessman and that he felt he would learn more by teaching Guido than by taking lessons from Olivi.

But what in reality does he 'teach' Guido? 'Seppi che a me sarebbe toccato non solo di regolare dei particolari come la corrispondenza e la contabilità, ma anche di sorvegliare gli affari'(II,ii, *823*). [I knew it would devolve on me to arrange such details as the correspondence and the accounts, as well as keeping an eye on the business generally.] There is in fact no attempt on his part to 'sorvegliare gli affari'. He takes no active part in the business and his advice is limited to counselling activity and caution in the most unhelpfully generic terms. At critical moments, as during the copper sulphate transaction, he is away from the office; consequently his negligence is a not inconsiderable factor in Guido's failure. By using such phrases as 'la nostra perdita' (II,ii, *836*) [our losses] he seems at times to imply an identity of interests which did not exist, as he makes clear two paragraphs later when he states that he can feel no responsibility for Guido's losses. There is, too, a continual insistence on Zeno's part that he has no talent for business, an assertion which has a curious ring about it in the light of the final chapter. His talent and luck are such that he is able, as Ada says, to ensure that Guido died 'proprio per una cosa che non ne valeva la pena' (II,ii, *922*) [for something that was not worth the trouble]. This is not to say, of course, that Zeno is solely responsible for Guido's ruin and death; in the words of the modern decalogue he did not kill, but he did not 'strive officiously to keep alive'.

Zeno sees and hears reproaches everywhere – in Carmen's eyes, in the dead Guido's face, as well as in Ada's accusations. He asserts too often and too forcibly that these accusations were false, that Guido's reproaches were not directed at him but at the rest of the family, who had encouraged him to gamble on the Stock Exchange. There are too many indications of his antipathy for Guido for one to take at face value either these protestations of innocence or his claim that he regarded Guido as a weakling in need of a protection which he willingly gave him. On the other hand, Zeno's account of events is the 'truth' in the sense in which he uses the word; he could not tell his story differently, and his inner compulsions make him believe his own fictions.

One of the most powerful impulses behind Zeno's writing is undoubtedly the need to prove himself innocent. His reaction to his father's death is 'Egli era morto ed io non potevo più provargli la mia innocenza!' (II,ii, *645*) [He was dead and it was impossible for me to prove my innocence.] And when, after Guido's funeral, Ada goes ro join her parents-in-law in South America, Zeno watches the liner leave and reflects: 'Ecco ch'essa ci abbandonava e che mai più avrei potuto provarle la mia innocenza' (II, ii, *926*). [She was leaving us for ever. Never again should I be able to prove to her that I was innocent.] with which revealing words the main part of Zeno's memoirs ends. His *malaise*, in other words, has a moral origin; his search for a cure is in reality a search for a disease on which he can blame his shortcomings. Sartre has argued in *L'Être et le néant* that we are always conscious of the unconscious and that to disclaim responsibility for it – as Zeno appears to be attempting to – is 'bad faith'; this may be true of our post-Freudian age, although Freud had anticipated the point, but in any case Zeno is the child of an earlier age and is convincingly represented as having difficulty in reconciling himself to the notion of an unconscious which is not accessible to introspection.

Is Zeno cured? One's answer to this question will depend on one's interpretation of the final section, *Psico-analisi*, in which Zeno, instead of accepting the analyst's diagnosis with due awe and gratitude and then going on to a process of re-education, rejects it. He gives up his treatment and ridicules a diagnosis which he claims was based on incomplete and inaccurate information. He claims that introspection has made him worse, not better, and that his commercial activities during the absence of Olivi – who as an Italian citizen had to leave Trieste during the war – have cured him.

Svevo possibly had in mind when writing this chapter a conversation between Levin and Koznyshev in Tolstoy's *Anna Karenin*. Levin lives on his estate and devotes himself to farming. He tells his brother, 'You would hardly believe how good this kind of thing is for every sort of foolishness. I am thinking of enriching medicine with a new term: *Arbeitskur* – health through work!'

'Well, certainly you don't need it much, it seems to me.'

'No, but those who suffer with their nerves do.'[4] It is this reference to nerves that makes *Anna Karenin* a more likely source than *The Sorrows of Young Werther* or *Faust*.

Alongside this passage and others like it one could quote Svevo's essay *Un individualista* (1886), in which he approvingly quotes Taine's opinion that 'l'unica felicità durevole sia riservata all'uomo nel lavoro collettivo' (III, *605*) [the only lasting happiness reserved for man is in collective work]. Health and satisfaction through work might seem to be a satisfactory philosophy on which to base the conclusion of a novel, but one has also to remember that this was not in the end enough of a philosophy for Levin and that between Tolstoy and Svevo there had come the debased and misunderstood versions of Nietzsche's Superman to which Svevo refers in his letter of 10

December 1927. 'E perché voler curar la nostra malattia? Davvero dobbiamo togliere all'umanità quello ch'essa ha di meglio? Io credo sicuramente che il vero successo che mi ha dato la pace è consistito in questa convinzione. Noi siamo una vivente protesta contro la ridicola concezione del superuomo come ci è stata gabellata (soprattutto a noi italiani)' (I, *859–60*). [Why wish to cure our illness? Must we really deprive humanity of the best thing it has? I firmly believe that the real success that has given me peace lies in this conviction. We are a living protest against the absurd concept of the Superman as it has been passed off to us (especially to us Italians).] This is probably a reference to D'Annunzio, Mussolini and Fascism, but it contains the important idea that certain kinds of 'health' are harmful and conversely that certain kinds of illness represent man's hope for the future. In that the Superman was to transcend the common man, whom Nietzsche regarded as a 'disease', Svevo can be seen as conducting a consistent polemic against Nietzsche. It is not these considerations alone, however, which lead one to reject Zeno's claim to be cured, and even to suggest that it is misleading of him to present the issue in those terms.

After pouring scorn on the doctor, Zeno goes on to construct a new version of his past which it is impossible to reconcile with anything he has told us so far: 'Io chiudo gli occhi e vedo subito puro, infantile, ingenuo il mio amore per mia madre, il mio rispetto ed il grande mio affetto per mio padre' (II, ii, *928*). [I have but to close my eyes and immediately there rises up before me my love for my mother, and the great respect and affection I felt for my father.] This is unacceptable because Zeno has hitherto consistently described his relationship with his father in terms of antagonism and feelings alternating between superiority and inferiority. This transfiguration of the past is later carried several stages further, and Zeno offers his life as an ideal against which 'normal' life is judged and found wanting. 'Com'era stata più bella la mia vita che non quella dei cosidetti sani, coloro che picchiavano o avrebbero voluto picchiare la loro donna ogni giorno salvo in certi momenti. Io, invece, ero stato accompagnato sempre dall'amore ...' (II, ii, *941*). [How much better my life had been than that of the so-called normal healthy man who, except at certain moments, beats or would like to beat his mistress every day. But I had always been accompanied by love.] Thus harmony, which Zeno longs for but cannot attain, is once more seen as the alternative to the competitive society.

Svevo posts enough clues at this point to guide his reader towards his meaning, especially as Zeno now chooses to support his argument by some thoroughly bad logic, although it is as usual interspersed with occasional flashes of insight, as when he perceives that countertransference has taken place. He argues, for example, that he cannot have had an Oedipus complex because he has not been cured of it, which is a splendidly circular argument. It is at this stage in the first part of the final chapter, dated 3 May 1915, that Zeno makes his celebrated statement that 'Una confessione in iscritto è sempre menzognera. Con ogni nostra parola toscana noi mentiamo' (II, ii, 928). [A written confession is always mendacious. We lie with every word we speak in the Tuscan tongue!] He then goes on to explain, in writing and in Tuscan, that the information he had given to Dr S. was incorrect and inadequate. He also attributes his illness to his treatment, which is an interesting half-truth since patients in the course of analysis are liable to feel worse before they begin to improve.

By 15 May, Zeno is beginning to feel better. Writing is having its desired therapeutic effect, and his new view of his past is confirmed to his own satisfaction. We are also introduced to what is to become a central theme in Svevo's later work – that of old age and the need to keep sexual desire alive for as long as possible. Infidelity is thus justified as a form of hygiene.

War now separates Zeno from his family, and we begin to see that the dating of the action of the novel, and particularly of the final chapter, is as crucial as that of Musil's *Man without Qualities* and its 'Emperor of peace' campaign. What Italian could overlook that it was precisely on the day of Italy's entry into the war, and in an area which was to see much bitter fighting, that Zeno, as concerned as ever with provoking in others a response which he can find agreeable, assured Teresina and her father that there would be no war there? His irresponsible reason for doing so is that he likes to see people happy and enjoing themselves. And is not war-time Trieste a strange place in which to achieve peace of mind?

There is much ambiguity in Zeno's statement that

> La guerra mi prese, mi squassò come un cencio, mi privò in una sola volta di tutta la mia famiglia ed anche del mio amministratore. Da un giorno all'altro io fui un uomo del tutto nuovo, anzi per essere più esatto, tutte le mie ventiquattr'ore furono nuove del tutto. Da ieri sono un po' più calmo perché finalmente, dopo l'attesa di un mese, ebbi le prime notizie della mia famiglia. Si trova sana e salva a Torino mentre io già avevo perduto ogni speranza di rivederla (II, ii, 944). [The war took hold of me,

shook me out like a rag, and robbed me at one blow of all my family, including my steward. From one day to the next I became a completely new man or, to be more exact, every one of my twenty-four hours was different. Since yesterday I have felt a little calmer, for after waiting a whole month I have at last had news of my family. They are safe and sound at Turin, while I had already lost all hope of seeing them again.]

Zeno would presumably have us believe that his improved state of mind is that of the benevolent *pater familias* and employer who is relieved to know that his family and principal employee are safe. We should accept this explanation if we had earlier been given some evidence that Zeno was such a laudable personage. Since we have not, we look for some other explanation of his conduct and tentatively conclude that his relief may derive from the certainty that separation is more or less irrevocable, at least for the foreseeable future. The war has removed Dr S., thus giving Zeno the perfect excuse for breaking with him completely. It has also removed and rendered powerless Olivi, that perpetual reminder of his father's power and authority, whom he can now ridicule. 'L'Olivi dalla Svizzera mi fece pervenire dei consigli. Se sapesse come i suoi consigli stonano in quest'ambiente ch'è mutato del tutto' (II, ii, 952). [Olivi sends me good advice from Switzerland. If only he knew how inappropriate it is to these surroundings, where everything is entirely changed!] War has also removed Augusta, squinting Jocasta to his limping Oedipus. Zeno's symptoms have been temporarily alleviated by a greater disorder in society at large, and the novel thus acquires overtones of wider significance relating to the state of society.

Zeno naturally seeks an explanation for his improved condition, and finds it in commerce, but his explanation of how this came about is so confused that he seems to be saying both 'Commerce has cured me' and 'I can engage in commerce because I am no longer ill', which is rather like saying 'I can take medicine because I am no longer ill'. In any case it would be unwise to build too ambitious a critical edifice on the foundations of Zeno's commercial activities. There is a moment when Zeno, returning from Lucinico, is hailed by a friend : 'Hai preso parte ai saccheggi?' (II, ii, 952) [Have you been taking part in the sack too?] The question is gently ironical; the speaker does not really believe that so respectable a citizen as Zeno Cosini would have taken part in the looting, mainly by Italians of the working class, which marked Italy's declaration of war against Austria. Nevertheless, if he had been pressed for a reply, he would have been compelled to answer, 'Not yet!' The looting prefigures his commercial activities, which are those of a war profiteer. Zeno has neither inserted himself into society nor achieved detachment from it; he has discovered that the unusual circumstances prevailing allow him to give full rein to his aggressive instincts. Not for nothing does he talk of his activities in terms of 'struggle' and 'victory' in language reminiscent of that used earlier to describe his feelings during the walk back to Trieste after missing Guido Speier's funeral. 'Ammetto che per avere la persuasione della salute il mio destino dovette mutare e scaldare il mio organismo con la lotta e sopratutto col trionfo' (II, ii, *953*). [I admit that my fate had to change, and my body to be warmed up by fighting and above all by victory, before I arrived at the conviction that I was well.] 'Mi paragonavo col povero Guido e salivo, salivo in alto con la mia vittoria nella stessa lotta nella quale egli era soggiaciuto' (II, ii, *919*). [I compared myself with poor Guido, and rose victorious from the same battle in which he lay vanquished.] There is remarkable similarity in mood, tone and vocabulary. There is also a significant difference. Guido as a term of comparison is no longer relevant; Zeno feels privileged and successful by comparison with the whole war-stricken city, and this is the main source of his 'health', deny it how he will.

But if Zeno is all these things – egoist, liar, adulterer, sadist and finally war profiteer – why is it so difficult, even in spite of a natural Anglo-Saxon censoriousness, totally to disapprove of him? It is not simply, I believe, that his humour is engaging and his optimism – his incorrigible, unwarranted optimism, purchased with illusion and the sacrifice of truth – is infectious. Nor is it merely that I must, if I am honest, confess to a sneaking feeling of envy towards a man who seems to be able in so many ways to have his cake and eat it. For Zeno is incessantly haunted by feelings of guilt which no-one else seems to share for behaviour which the society in which he lives finds tolerable. If Darwin, Marx and Spencer were right, society existed in a state of conflict; the victors were applauded for their triumphs. Zeno, too, has triumphed, but the fruits of victory turn sour in his mouth and he needs to explain his tactics away. He does so by constructing out of words a 'passato che più non duole' (II, ii, *927*) [a past that is no longer hateful to me] and also by suggesting that he cannot be blamed for his success since he has achieved it in spite of his blunders. He implies continually that he is what in Jewish culture would be known as a *schlemiel*.

The *schlemiel* is a stock Jewish character. He had a long history in Jewish, and especially Yiddish, lore before he made his first significant appearance in European literature in Adalbert von Chamisso's *Peter Schlemihls wundersame Geschichte* (1814). The *schlemiel* is a fool; not charming, wily or saintly, but weak, inept and frequently disliked. In spite of his vices, or the humiliations he may suffer, he is a comic hero and his humour is used in self-defence. He bases his life on the assumption that because he is absurd he cannot be tragic, and thus he retains a capacity for hope in circumstances which would drive other men to despair. He tries to convince us that his weakness is really strength. Sometimes he may succeed, but as often as not his 'victories' are presented ironically by a narrator who retains an awareness of reality which his character has lost.

Svevo's familiarity with German literature, and particularly the works of Heine, means that he knew the *schlemiel*, and one can find him casting himself in the rôle of *schlemiel* in some of his letters to his wife, which occasionally read like preliminary sketches of episodes for *La coscienza di Zeno*. It is difficult to read the letters of 1 June 1901 (1, 253) or 5 April 1906 (1, 435–7) without being reminded of the mostly untrue stories which Zeno tells to the Malfenti sisters, or his account of the table-turning episode.

That Zeno is a highly individual but nevertheless recognizable variation on a stock Jewish type may account for one otherwise puzzling aspect of Svevo's reputation and reception. He has never been a widely popular author, and the English editions of his works sell in quantities which have disappointed their publishers, mainly because his kind of irony is not widely understood in England. The situation in the United States, however, is quite different. *Senilità* and *La coscienza di Zeno* have been reprinted several times in American editions. The reason for this seems to be that there is in America a substantially larger Jewish population than in England and there are also several American novelists – Saul Bellow, Isaac Rosenfeld, B.J. Friedman and others – whose characters are cast in the same mould as Zeno. The *schlemiel* has enjoyed a remarkable vogue in American fiction during the last thirty years,[5] to which Svevo, together with novelists such as Scholom Aleichem, have, I think, contributed significantly.

The *schlemiel* is sometimes seen as an embodiment of the technique of adaptation required of the Jew if he is to survive. In the most recent stage of his evolution he seems also to have become a device by means of which the narrator passes an implicit and unfavourable verdict on the society which has produced him. Commenting on a number of such characters in recent American fiction, Wisse states that 'Each is maimed – ulcerous, fat, or neurotic – yet interpreted as an example of relative health. There is about them a touch of cheerfulness, unwarranted by the facts of the case, but there nonetheless.' This does not apply completely to Zeno, whose cheerfulness, as he pockets the proceeds of his speculations in war-stricken Trieste, is morally offensive. But if, on the other hand, we consider his optimism in conjunction with his other qualities – and his lack of qualities – may we not see here a way to resolve the ambiguity of our reactions to him? And by the same token we may see that the conclusion of the novel is neither crassly optimistic nor totally pessimistic.

Maxia, in relation to *La coscienza*, appropriately cites the essay *L'uomo e la teoria darwiniana*, in which Svevo argues that most men, fortunately for themselves and for the stability of the social order, stop developing. They adapt successfully to the demands of the struggle for life, and their adaptation gives them 'un sentimento di superiorità ed anche una superiorità di forza reale' (III, *638*) [a feeling of superiority and a truly superior strength], but from the point of view of evolution they are, as it were, a blind alley: the future, in Svevo's view, lies as it does in Musil, with the man without qualities. 'Nella mia mancanza assoluta di uno sviluppo marcato in qualsivoglia senso', Svevo goes on, 'io sono quell'uomo. Lo sento tanto bene che nella mia solitudine me ne glorio altamente e sto aspettando sapendo di non essere altro che un abbozzo' (III, *638*). [Completely lacking a pronounced development in any direction whatever, I am that man. I am so sure of it that in my solitude I glory in the fact and wait, knowing that I am just a rough draft.] The next section of the essay introduces the idea of man's 'ordigni', devices or tools which constitute a new kind of evolution apart from that of the body, guided always by man's restless spirit.

These ideas are taken further in the essay *La corruzione dell'anima*, in which Svevo clarifies further what he means by 'ordigni'. They were tools and implements in the early stages of evolution, but Svevo now enlarges the meaning of the word, as Marx had done, to include concepts and systems of thought.

> Alcuni di questi ordigni erano idee. La giustizia che regola le avventure e le sventure attenuendole o aggravandole, la scienza ch'è l'espressione più alta dell'anima malcontenta, che prepara gli ordigni e crea il loro bisogno, la religione che dà qualche istante di pace all'anima torva e infine l'ordinamento sociale e econimico cioè un metodo per far convivere in una guerra dall' aspetto di pace il triste e malvagio animale guerresco' (III, *643*).

[Some of these tools were ideas. Justice, which regulates adventures and misadventures, mitigating or aggravating them; science, which is the highest expression of the discontented spirit, which prepares tools and creates the need for them; religion, which gives an occasional moment of peace to the surly spirit; and lastly, the social and economic order, which is a means of making the evil, malevolent and warlike animal live in a state of war which looks peaceful.]

Svevo seems to be revising evolutionary theory in the light of Hegel's *The Phenomonology of the Spirit* (1807). Thus is why his Darwinism, with its fable of the survival of man as a parasite, seems unorthodox; but others before Svevo had attempted a synthesis of Hegelian thought and Darwinism. Nor was the enterprise at all misguided. The theory of the evolution of the species, although rejected by Hegel because it had no foundation in the science of his time, fits in very well with his philosophy of an evolving nature, with the guiding 'spirit' as the philosophic equivalent of natural selection. What Svevo did was to take the new scientific principle of natural selection and describe it in terms of the survival, not of the fittest but, following a suggestion in Hegel, of the basest.

The source of this original twist to evolutionary theory is that part of the *Phenomonology* in which Hegel comments on Diderot's *Le Neveu de Rameau*, and which has recently been discussed by Lionel Trilling in *Sincerity and Spontaneity* (1972). Hegel could see in *Le Neveu de Rameau* the contrast between the narrator, the *Diderot-moi*, and Rameau's shifty nephew, a man without qualities. Hegel sees the former as the 'honest soul', a man who is content to be what he is and to show others what he is, and who can regard the institutions and authorities of the society in which he lives with respect; the latter is all things to all men, a 'disintegrated consciousness', and is seen as 'base'. But the very qualities which lead conventional morality to approve of the 'honest soul' lead Hegel to reject him since he is limited by his very relationship to society. The 'base soul', on the other hand, is accepted because he incarnates the attempts of the Spirit to resist the restrictions imposed on it by the conventions of 'honest' society.

Zeno Cosini is, in Hegelian terms, a 'disintegrated consciousness'; in literary terms he is a direct descendant of Rameau's nephew. The 'coscienza' of the novel's title thus has yet another layer of meaning. Zeno's lack of qualities and bonds with society make him open to the future in a way which ensures at least the possibility of development. His rejection of a 'cure' through analysis is therefore a lucky escape, since Freudianism is seen here as a highly sophisticated form of determinism, the aim of which is to make the 'base soul' conform to socially acceptable patterns and so stultify his growth. Svevo's version of evolutionary theory thus stands in contrast to that of Nietzsche, who in *Thus Spake Zarathustra* and *Ecce Homo* predicted that evolution would lead merely to the 'last man', who would be an uncreative conformist and hedonist. (Is Guido Speier Svevo's 'last man'? one wonders.) Nietzsche proposed instead the Superman, who would rise above conventional morality. Svevo, however, finds the irrational, in this Dionysian manifestation, morally reprehensible; the 'base soul' who in a sense sinks below conventional morality, is another matter.

Augusta's 'healthy' instincts and artless honesty, which seem at first only to offer a yard-stick by which to measure Zeno and find him wanting, are in reality her condemnation. Zeno compares her to the swallow building her nest and to the ant preparing for winter, and these similes are not merely decorative; they are a clear indication that although she is perfectly adjusted to her function as wife and mother and to her station in society she has, like the animals in the essays, lost her 'anima' and presents no possibilities for the future of evolution. She is Hegel's 'honest soul', living unreservedly in the present and regarding the authorities of her society with respect and tranquillity as guardians of her world.

When, however, did Svevo write these essays on Darwinism? *L'uomo e la teoria darwiniana*, on internal evidence, must have been written after 1907, while the tone of the discussion of 'ordigni' and the social order in *La corruzione dell'anima* suggests that it must date from the First World War. The most important 'ordigni' mentioned in the latter are *ideas* – justice, religion, and the social and economic order, the function of which is to direct man's aggressive impulses into peaceful channels. Zeno, too, in the final paragraphs of the novel, talks of man's 'ordigni', and his account of them reveals the extent to which Svevo's thought has been modified by the war. Health is now equated with that of the animals who know only the progress of their own organism; and the image of the swallow in this passage once again calls Augusta to mind as one of the few 'healthy' characters in the novel. Life – on-going life, prompted always by discontent – is constantly provoking new developments, always threatening the stable state in which the Augustas, the 'honest souls' of this world, live. It is in this sense that life, as Zeno puts it, is a disease of matter, for nothing is more stable than inert matter. But bespectacled man's discontent has led to the invention of 'ordigni' not discussed in the essays, destructive instruments of unprecedented power: by 1919 these have overshadowed in Svevo's mind man's other achievements. Man differs from other animals in that he has the capacity to destroy the species to which he belongs. Svevo thus poses in the starkest possible form the problem of aggression and man's almost unlimited capacity for destruction. In the light of this Zeno offers meagre comfort indeed.

7. Last Narrative Fiction, 1923-28

In 1925 Svevo told Valéry Larbaud that he had written nothing since the publication of *La coscienza di Zeno*. It is tempting to see in this silence a parallel to the period of withdrawal which followed the publication of *Senilità*. When Silvio Benco reviewed *La coscienza* in the Triestine newspaper *Il Piccolo della Sera*, Svevo wrote to thank him. 'Già lo sapevo', he wrote, 'che avrei trovato da Lei il conforto al grande dolore di aver pubblicato' (I, 747). [I was sure that I would find in you comfort for the great pain of publishing.] The 'dolore' grew greater as time passed and the reviews made it seem likely that not even with this novel was Svevo to achieve fame. Disappointment and pain were again the price of publication.

His mood is reflected in the short story or fable *La madre*, which he apparently began in 1910 but did not put into a final version until 1926. Curra is a chicken, hatched in an incubator, who goes in search of the mother he has never known, 'la madre di cui si diceva che sapesse procurare ogni dolcezza e perciò anche la soddisfazione dell'ambizione e della vanità' (III, *131*) [the mother who was said to be able to give every blessing and therefore also to satisfy ambition and vanity]. He thinks he has found her in the next garden, but when he takes the worm which she has found for her brood, she rounds on him and drives him out as an intruder. Later, still convinced that she was his mother, Curra reflects bitterly that it would have been better for him had he never known her. I find the suggestion that the real subject of the story is Svevo's (hypothetical) castration complex unconvincing and prefer the conventional view that the fierce hen whose care is all for her own chicks and will not provide food for one who has strayed in from next door is Italy, or the Italian critics; the bewildered Curra is Svevo, his garden Trieste; that he should return to *La madre* after the publication of *La coscienza* suggests a return to a state of mind similar to that which had originally inspired it.

There is another factor which would explain a period of silence after *La coscienza*. Svevo had found his use of the first-person narrator very demanding. He had tried to think and feel, even to walk and smoke, like Zeno, and after the effort involved in doing this while writing a work of such length and complexity he may have needed time in which to rest before undertaking another large-scale work. Certainly he resolved at this stage never to use the technique again on the grounds that it was too demanding, which may well account in part for the use of an omniscient third-person narrator in *Corto viaggio sentimentale*, which he began in London in 1925.

Corto viaggio sentimentale was intended to be a long short story rather than a full-length novel. It describes a journey from Milan to Trieste made by the elderly Signor Aghios, who has with him thirty thousand lire in banknotes which he had intended to convert into a money order for the sake of convenience. He enjoys travelling since it enables him to feel free and uncommitted, to enter into superficially friendly relationships with strangers who make no demands on him and to whom he can freely lie and tell the anecdotes with which his family is familiar. In many ways he resembles Zeno. He is a compulsive liar and has a sense of irony. He has, like Zeno, an apocalyptic vision, which has lost none of its immediacy, of the world becoming one vast city. He likes to be surrounded by goodwill at no cost to himself. He befriends a fellow traveller, a young man named Bacis who is encouraged by Aghios's benevolence (and wealth) to explain that he needs fifteen thousand lire to enable him to put his complicated emotional life in order and make himself free to marry his true love. Aghios listens; but confronted with real need his theoretical benevolence fades away and we see that his name, which puns on the Greek for *saint*, is used ironically. In Venice he takes Bacis with him when he goes to see the jeweller Meuli, and he tells the young man how he had befriended the jeweller, who had then cheated him out of a large sum of money which he had subsequently recovered. He bears Meuli no ill-will, and his story sets a pattern to which Bacis conforms, for while Aghios is asleep in the train the young lover robs him of fifteen thousand lire; an honest thief, he takes no more than he said he needed. One wonders how the story would have ended. Would Aghios have convinced himself that he had given the money to Bacis? Or would Bacis have been denounced to the police by another traveller, the officious Borlini, whose unthinking belief in law and order and a strong government seems to imply a veiled criticism of Fascism? 'Justice' would thus be done and Aghios, his defensive barriers intact, would then be free to indulge in compassion at no cost to himself: and cheap compassion is another form of self-indulgence.

But *Corto viaggio sentimentale* remained unfinished, and whatever

Svevo may have said about not writing again in the first person, Zeno was still there, waiting. *La coscienza di Zeno*, as critics have frequently remarked, is an 'open work' – not, I believe, in the sense that the reader is free to complete it how he will but in the sense that it catches the fluidity of life itself, which we know will go on after we have read the final page. Since the novel ends in 1916, with Zeno rather improbably on the crest of a wave, one naturally wonders what happens next. Especially one wonders this if one believes that Zeno's position at the end of the novel is only provisional, the result of a temporary and fortuitous combination of circumstances.

Quite at what point Svevo returned to Zeno we do not know. *Le confessioni del vegliardo* (III, 492) is a brief one-page fragment of a novel of which the central character was to be a certain Giovanni Respiro who was born on the same day as Svevo – 19 December 1861 – and who starts in his old age to write his memoirs. The form was thus to have combined both first- and third-person narrators, but the disadvantage of the method was that Respiro would naturally begin by remembering his childhood, which would echo *La coscienza* too closely and not allow Svevo to progress much beyond the stage he had reached in the earlier novel. *Le confessioni* is therefore a false start.

Il vecchione (III, 133–42), generally assigned to 1928, is another false start. In 1925, when his French friends had attracted the attention of French (and, indirectly, of Italian) literary circles to *La coscienza*, Svevo had been compared to Proust. The comparison is misleading, since the differences between them are more important than what they have in common, but *Il vecchione* seems to have been written after a reading of Proust. Zeno, narrating in the first person and now rather older, relates an incident which occurred when he and Augusta were returning by car from Capodistria on a hot day. Waking suddenly from his sleep Zeno sees and greets a pretty girl. When Augusta asks who she is, Zeno gives a name, only for Augusta to point out that the 'girl' he has named must now be as old as himself. Zeno's 'mémoire volontaire' gets things wrong; time itself is confused, and the days, months and years break their orderly ranks once they are out of our sight. Zeno then re-reads his earlier memoirs, intending to continue them.

This section of the novel is unfinished, but what were to be the central themes are introduced. Zeno writes in order to feel alive, to understand himself – or so he tells us – and also as a form of hygiene. There is also an interesting disquisition on the nature of time. Health, old age, and the idealization of life through writing – these are the preoccupations of Svevo's last fiction.

The real start and the main body of Svevo's last novel consist of four sections, *Le confessioni del vegliardo* (III, 372–404), *Umbertino* (III, 405–34), *Il mio ozio* (III, 435–53), and *Un contratto* (III, 454–74). The first begins in much more simple and direct fashion than *Il vecchione*: Zeno, dating his memoirs 4 April 1928 and characteristically regarding the date as the beginning of a new period in his life, relates that he has found and re-read his old memoirs and proposes to continue them.

The starting-point of his story is naturally the end of the war. The restoration of 'normality' tears down the defensive barriers Zeno had so carefully erected around himself in 1916. He has given up work, having proved considerably less successful in commerce than he had believed himself to be, and the son of his former administrator now manages his business. The main emphasis in this first section, however, is on Zeno's relations with his children. His son, Alfio, wants to be an artist, claims to be a Communist, and finds his father too inclined to laugh at everything. Zeno sees his son's rebellious tendencies as a manifestation of weakness, and when he looks at his son's paintings, the modern style of which he dislikes, he can even manage to convince himself that he, Zeno, is the most stable and judicious member of his family. His efforts to bridge the generation gap are as unavailing as were his father's, and he reflects with some relish that his own death will be as much of a punishment for Alfio as was his father's for himself.

Zeno's daughter Antonia is a widow, and she and her son, Umbertino, live with Zeno and Augusta. The way in which her grief is seen by her father as a constant irritant reveals his egoism. David Storey's Pasmore, in the novel of the same name (1972), is a similar, albeit less complex, character. But at this stage Antonia is a secondary character, introduced partly as a foil to Zeno and partly as a means of introducing Zeno's grandson.

The second section of the novel shows Zeno learning 'l'art d'être grand-père'. The account of the at times disturbing impact of a very young child on the life and routine of a self-centred old man is vivid, even moving at times. Yet in spite of its title, much of this section is concerned not with Umbertino but with his mother and the problems, as Zeno sees them, of having a widowed daughter in the house – especially one who seems to have inherited some of her father's qualities. 'Tanti ereditano dal padre il naso lungo mal disegnato e lasciano ai fratelli la bella statura o gli occhi espressivi. A lei toccava i miei rimorsi da lei tanto più insopportabili perché del tutto irragionevoli' (III, 424). [So many children inherit from their father his long, ugly nose, while his fine physique or expressive eyes go to their brothers and sisters. Antonietta inherited my remorses, which were all the more unbearable for her, being completely irrational.] The implication of that statement is that he at least had good cause to feel remorse.

Another character who could have acquired a certain importance is Zeno's nephew Carlo, the son of Guido Speier. He tends to make fun of his elderly uncle, and because he puts their relationship on an undemanding level, Zeno is fond of him. He even describes him as the first person with whom he has been sincere in his whole life; but when he adds 'Fui sincero con Carlo benché non interamente' (III, 427) [But sincere though I was with Carlo, I was not wholly sincere], the warning is clear. 'Sincerity' is about to undergo the same change in meaning as so many other words in Zeno's vocabulary.

The introduction of Carlo, who is also a doctor, leads naturally to the next section, *Il mio ozio*, the central themes of which are Zeno's declining health and the various stratagems by which he hopes to cheat nature, which he believes will suppress those she no longer considers to be capable of reproduction. Illness and death are seen as inevitable and natural, not the result of disorder, and 'health' is now defined as the progressive and simultaneous decline of all the organs. Zeno tries twice to 'cheat' nature. He considers undergoing one of those rejuvenation operations which were fashionable in the 1920s and 1930s, and he also takes a young mistress. The operation is a splendid example of Svevo's use of 'pseudo-science', for Zeno believes in its efficacy for a time even though his creator does not. The affair with Felicita echoes his affair with Carla in that it too is governed by financial considerations and Zeno's avarice. Nor, in view of the part played in Zeno's life by smoking, should one overlook the fact that Felicita and her brother own a cigarette kiosk.

Zeno's relationship with Felicita had in a sense been a contractual one, since he took out a regular subscription for her services. *Un contratto* deals with another contractual relationship, that with his new administrator. Zeno's experience and advice are no longer relevant in the changed post-war world. The family business goes badly until young Olivi reorganizes it; but he only does so after he has manœuvred his employer into giving him a new contract which assures him an increased salary and fifty per cent of the profits. Zeno regards the contract as a defeat at the hands of the younger generation but enjoys the irony of a situation in which the socialist Olivi works for a capitalist and even reduces the workers' wages.

Here is the clearest indication of the novelty of the unfinished work. Many of its themes – sincerity, the effect of money on personal relationships, egoism – will seem familiar, but Zeno is now on the older side of the generation gap and sees the problems of heredity and the relations between the generations in a totally new perspective. *Le confessioni*, even in its unfinished state, is an original and thoughtful contribution to the literature of old age. Then why did it remain unfinished?

Svevo several times complained in his last years that the difficulty at his age lay not in starting but in finishing. No doubt it is true to say that he died before he could finish the novel; but might not this statement be a mere tautology – as if one were to say that it is unfinished because he never finished it – concealing another, and more important, truth? *Le confessioni* is by its very nature an unfinishable novel. It is an illuminating study of the tensions, inner conflicts and regrets which lie beneath the seemingly placid surface of the daily life of an old man who admits that he thinks more about the past than the future. He admits, too, that he corrects, even falsifies, the past. This implies that Zeno has achieved a greater measure of self-knowledge than before; one cannot imagine him making a statement like that in 1915 or 1916. But as is so often the case with Zeno, one truth is used to conceal another. Zeno's mind *is* very much on the future, and the key event of the novel, which casts its shadow over all that comes before it, is one which the novel can never be allowed to reach.

The dilemma is hinted at in the opening paragraphs of *Le confessioni*, in which Zeno reflects, as he reads the pages he wrote earlier and muses on those he is about to write, that he will have the surprise of finding himself different from the Zeno of his previous memoirs. He says he no longer has the terrible fear of the future he had then, since he is now living that future, which is in its turn departing, but without making way for another future. 'Perciò non è neppure un vero presente, sta fuori del tempo. Manca un tempo ultimo nella grammatica' (III, 373). [So it is not even a *bona-fide* present. It is outside time. Grammar does not possess a *final* tense.] Of course the statement that Zeno is not afraid of the future is false; death is never far from his mind, but it is the one event he will not be able to render harmless by converting in into 'literature'. Can one imagine *La morte di mio padre* narrated by the father?

Death is also the central theme of the story *Proditoriamente*, in which the elderly Signor Maier is made to realize that his bankruptcy is insignificant in the light of the death of the friend from whom he had hoped to borrow money; and the unfinished tale *La morte* deals with the death of an elderly man who had expected his wife to die first. Svevo's most satisfactory completed works of these last years, however, are the two long stories *La novella del buon vecchio e della bella fanciulla*, and *Una burla riuscita*.

La novella del buon vecchio, generally thought to have been written in 1926, deals with an old man who takes a young mistress in order to cheat nature. This is also the theme of *Il mio ozio*, and in so far as the protagonists of both works are also writers there is a similarity between them. The differences are more important than the similarities, however. In the *Novella* the old man overdoes his 'cure' and so exposes himself to nature's revenge, which takes the form of angina pectoris. He begins a dissertation on the subject of the relations between the young and the old, and in so doing he is guilty of an act of intellectual dishonesty which enables him to generalize and so to mis-state the issue, which is that he, a wealthy man in war-time Trieste, has taken advantage of his position to seduce a girl who was not well off. By setting his story in 1918 Svevo has given it an added historical and social dimension. It is true that the girl is very willing to be seduced, because of her financial situation, but the adjective 'buono' which Svevo uses to qualify the old man is fiercely ironical; his philanthropic pose emphasizes rather than conceals an egoism so monstrous that he can regard the girl merely as an object to be purchased, and resent the sound of distant gunfire as an obstacle to sleep. 'Perché non hanno ancora inventato il modo di ammazzarsi senza fare tanto chiasso?' (III, 34) [Why haven't they yet found a way of killing each other without making so much noise about it?] The old man's attitude towards the war is ambivalent; he feels remorse at making so much money out of it, and shame at his remorse. His 'philanthropy' towards the girl is intended to justify his continued profiteering.

The return in the *Novella* to a third-person narrative technique enables Svevo to fill out the picture of the girl rather more than would have been the case had he been using the first person. Even though attention is focussed mainly on the old man we are made aware of the ease with which the girl surrenders to him and of the way in which, in the course of the story, she quickly ascends the social ladder, becoming both more sophisticated and less scrupulous. Svevo's criticism is directed at her as well as at her lover. The narrator makes more, and more hostile, comments than in any other of his works. This is one of the bleakest stories Svevo ever wrote: he extends no compassion towards either of his characters, and if at the beginning there are circumstances which mitigate our condemnation of the girl, there are none at the end, and Svevo's verdict is that a willingness to be corrupted is almost as offensive as the desire to corrupt, although both are the result of an economic situation.

The end of the war provides the background to *Una burla riuscita*, a tale which could have been written only by an author with Svevo's sense of humour and an awareness of the workings of the international money market. The central character of the story is Mario Samigli, the elderly author of an unsuccessful novel who bears a remarkable likeness to Emilio Brentani. Samigli, who now writes only fables, is told by a colleague that the representative of a Viennese publisher is in Trieste and wishes to buy the translation rights of his novel. Everything hinges upon the fact that the day of the hoax is 3 November 1918, the day on which Italian troops disembarked in Trieste and when Austrian citizens had to leave. On this confused day Samigli meets the supposed representative, signs a false contract and receives in exchange a cheque which another colleague pays into the bank for him. The bank gives him a receipt stating that it had that day purchased from him two hundred thousand crowns at the current rate of exchange. When Samigli discovers the hoax he attacks his tormentor in a grotesque bout of fisticuffs. Later he discovers that because of the fluctuations in the exchange rate the hoax has brought him a profit of seventy thousand lire. But he is not enough of a dreamer to be able to see the money as a reward for his literary labours.

The narrator's attitude towards Samigli is rather less harsh than it was towards the old man, no doubt because he is sinned against as well as sinning, but he does not escape unscathed. His relationship with an invalid brother, whom he neglects, shows him to be remarkably self-centred, and he allows himself to be affected by the way in which values slide during this extraordinary and unstable period. The fluctuations in the exchange rate have an ironically symbolic value. There is nothing new, however, about the picture of Samigli as a 'sognatore'; in fact the mental processes of the dreamer are stated much too explicitly at the beginning of the story instead of being allowed to emerge as the story progresses. And at times it progresses too slowly and in disjointed fashion.

Samigli's novel was entitled *Una giovinezza*. D. Oliva, reviewing Svevo's *Una vita* on 11 December 1892 in the *Corriere della Sera*, complained that the title was inaccurate: Svevo, he maintained, had not related the story of Nitti's life, but that of his brief youth, which had suicide as its epilogue. The criticism rankled. Samigli's name and the title of his novel point to Svevo himself, and the subject – the effect on an elderly author of the prospect of fame – suggests that Svevo was dealing in this tale with his own reactions to the celebrity which came to him in 1925, and with the fear that it might after all bring only disappointment. But to say this is to raise the question of the relationship in Svevo's work between autobiography and art.

8. Autobiography and Art

Svevo is in some ways a curiously uninventive author. He recalled James Joyce as saying that there was only one novel in any writer's pen and that anything he wrote after that would be more or less the same work in a different form. In his case, Svevo added, the one novel would be *Una vita* (1, *759–60*). He repeated this idea in 1927, when he sent a copy of *Una vita* to the critic Enrico Rocca with the comment that he had written only one novel in his life (1, *846*). This is not necessarily a weakness, and several other novelists have willingly subscribed to the notion that they work in terms of a limited number of themes. Pavese maintained that every great writer was 'splendidly monotonous'.

In the case of Svevo it is true that his main characters do have the generic resemblance to each other which has been the subject of so much comment. They find themselves trapped in similar situations and engaging in similar relationships. It is equally true that the circumstances of their lives often resemble those of their creator. They tend to be of the same age as Svevo at the time of writing and to come from the same social class as himself. They have, like him, aspirations to authorship. Nitti works in a bank, finding his work tedious and unsatisfying; Svevo, when he wrote *Una vita*, was employed by the Unionbank, and never seems to have found his work particularly congenial. Nitti's aspirations to authorship and his habit of spending his evenings at the Biblioteca Civica are a reflection of Svevo's own. Brentani, again, is much the same age as Svevo at the time of writing. His life is also divided between his dull, undemanding office job and his literary career, in the course of which he has so far produced some newspaper articles and a novel which few people have read. His enthusiasm for Wagner – he attends the first performance in Trieste of part of *The Ring of the Niebelungen* – parallels Svevo's admiration for the German composer.

It is, however, with Zeno that we can see the closest parallels between creator and creation. They are of much the same age; Zeno was born in 1857, Svevo in 1861, which makes the former, at the time of writing his memoirs, as old as the latter at the time of beginning the novel. Both belong to the upper middle class, since Svevo has now gone up in the world. Zeno's unfinished student days are an exuberant caricature of Svevo's disorganized studies and reading. Zeno's violin playing, which never reaches great heights because he, like Svevo, lacks manual dexterity, even his wistful aside about the acting career which he might have had, his smoking habit, his preoccupation with dates, his hypochondria and his imagined diabetes – all have their origin in Svevo's private life. The catalogue can be extended to the minor works. Erlis, in *Incontro di vecchi amici*, writes unfinished short stories – a nice touch, when one remembers how many Svevo never finished, including this one. Aghios, in *Corto viaggio sentimentale*, speaks English badly; Samigli, in *Una burla riuscita*, writes animal fables and has doubts about the style of his novel; Restori and Svevo share the same birthday. One can see the force of Jonard's comment that if ever there was a writer who talked of nothing but himself, it was Svevo. Spagnoletti, too, has written of a 'continuous self-portrait'. Even more points of contact between Svevo's life and works might be revealed by a full-length biography of the kind which we now lack.

Even more striking and significant is the way in which certain neurotic tendencies and psychological problems tend to recur in both Svevo and his characters. The diary of Elio Schmitz and Svevo's letters and diaries reveal a continual state of dissatisfaction and of inferiority. The despondent diary note of 19 December 1889 (III, *813–14*), written on his twenty-eighth birthday, states that 'Il malcontento mio, di me e degli altri non potrebbe essere maggiore'. [My dissatisfaction – with myself and other people – could not be greater.] Saccone sees this dissatisfaction as the autobiographical impulse behind Svevo's work, and the state of mind which produced *L'assassinio di Via Belpoggio* and *Una vita*. The diary entry is a moving document, referring with a total absence of self-pity to financial difficulties, to his hypochondria, to unrealized ambitions and his unhappiness with his work, and his acute sense of isolation. In his letters he refers repeatedly to the tendency to indulge in day-dreams which he reveals as a source of weakness in his protagonists. And he displays such an acute sense of the discrepancy between his characters' professed ideals and the realities of their conduct that it is difficult at times not to see an implied reference to an uncomfortable awareness of his own situation, as a Socialist and a critic of existing social structures writing – especially after his marriage – from within the comfort and security of the system which he wished to end. If he criticizes Brentani for never lifting a finger to realize his Socialist ideals, is he not also criticizing himself? And through Zeno and the 'buon vecchio' is he not also reproaching himself for the way in which he had profited from the war? One could point out in his defence that Svevo was as much a prisoner of his situation as anyone else and that he had relatively little freedom of choice. Something like this thought must have occurred to Svevo, who would no doubt have regarded it as a rather crude form of determinism; and we have already seen that his protagonists use determinism as an excuse when they wish to evade responsibility for their actions. It is difficult to escape the conclusion that the guilt feelings which haunt Zeno are, at least on that level, Svevo's own.

One can suggest that Svevo was using his fiction as a means of externalizing, and so transcending, certain problems which did not seem to admit of a solution. It was a way of coming to terms with them. In other words, writing is for Svevo a form of therapy. There were of course dangers in this approach to literature; talking or writing about problems all too easily becomes a substitute for coming to terms with them, as Svevo clearly realized, which is why he exposes the way in which his protagonists mis-state issues and falsify problems. In the opening paragraphs of *Le confessioni del vegliardo* Zeno muses on the way in which writing transfigures life, anticipating a situation in which everyone will write and 'la vita sarà letteraturizzata'. 'Il raccoglimento occuperà il massimo tempo che così sarà sottratto all'orrida vita vera' (III, 372). [Life will become literature. ... And contemplation will be the main business of the day, preserving it from the wretchedness of actual living.] Life is unpleasant; let us convert it into literature, that is, falsify it in order to make it more acceptable. This is clearly not Svevo's aim, however much it may be Zeno's.

But did Svevo's therapy work? Jonard and others have argued that if Svevo continued to write it must have been because the therapy was unsuccessful. The implicit analogy on which this argument is based is that of certain conditions which require a once-and-for-all operation, or one course of treatment. Not all ailments are of this kind, however; some treatments need constantly to be renewed if the patient's condition is not to deteriorate. Dialysis is a case in point. Here perhaps is a more appropriate analogy, and on this basis one could argue that Svevo perseveres with his cure precisely because it works. This is not to say that it does not have unpleasant side-effects which he had not foreseen, especially his disappointment at the lack of recognition given to him; but it is not difficult to find medical parallels to that situation too. In any case there are many precedents for an author writing a 'sick' book to restore his moral or psychological health; Goethe's *Sorrows of Young Werther* is the most celebrated example which comes to mind.

Svevo's interest in Freudianism and the impact of psychoanalysis on literary criticism – particularly in view of current trends in 'psychobiography'[1] – raise the question of the extent to which one can characterize or analyse an author on the evidence offered by his works. One is naturally tempted to speculate about Svevo's state of mind when writing and about the factors in his unconscious which shaped his work. But speculate, and perhaps not very profitably, is all we can do. Freud declined to help Arnold Zweig in his attempt to study Nietzsche's mental collapse on the grounds that he knew little or nothing about his sexual constitution, which with Nietzsche he thought was a complete enigma. Critics, especially those who in Joyce's phrase are 'Jung and easily Freudened', would do well to show a like caution. It has been suggested, for example, that *La madre* deals with a castration complex. But apart from Freud's generalized statement that there was often a connection between that complex and the Jewish circumcision rite, what evidence is there that Svevo suffered from such a complex? Only that which is provided by this particular interpretation of the story, which is to engage in a circular argument. One may feel that individual interpretations of this kind are absurd, but the point is not that a psychological study of Svevo's work is in itself ridiculous. It is rather that psychological criticism of this kind tends to be reductive; it fails to take into account other important factors. And it allows complete subjectivity on the part of the critic, who is usually more expert in literature than psychoanalysis.

Nor must one forget that Svevo's characters are the result of a consciously directed process of composition, and that he frequently derives his raw material from more than one source. This is not to deny the value of inspiration or the presence of factors in the unconscious which shape the forms in which it expresses itself, but I suspect that for men such as Svevo – and the state of his manuscripts confirms the suspicion – literary composition is more of a paste and scissors affair than is often supposed. And at this point one has to say that if Svevo is uninventive – even the episode of Guido Speier's funeral is said in his family to be based on fact – he is splendidly imaginative. Consider, for example, the episode in which Zeno has himself shut up in a clinic in order to cure his smoking habit. While there he imagines that his wife might be engaging in a love affair with the doctor, who he has noticed is young and handsome. For the first time since his marriage he is jealous. Now Svevo is a most economical writer and rarely wastes a good idea. The origin of this episode can be traced back to his letters to his wife. On at least two occasions when she was taking the baths at Salsomaggiore he wrote to ask whether her doctor was young or old (I, *155, 168*). And in 1899 he wrote to tell her than an acquaintance had been confined in a mental asylum, adding: 'A me – se toccasse una cosa simile – avrei per prima idea che mia moglie m'avesse fatto rinchiudere per liberarsi di me e morrei arrovellandomi dall'ira. Per la prima volta in mia vita avrei torto' (I, *146*). [If such a thing were to happen to me, my first thought would be that my wife had had me shut up in order to free herself of me, and I should die bursting with anger. For the first time in my life I should be wrong.] Svevo puts these incidents together, makes his and Zeno's common desire to give up smoking the motive for the latter's temporary incarceration, and the episode of Dr Muli's clinic is born. Or let us take the example of the death of Zeno's father. Svevo's authoritarian father does not seem to have had a high opinion of his son, for in 1915 Svevo wrote to his daughter: 'Sto diventando un uomo d'affari molto serio. Papa mio diceva che avrei messo giudizio a 40 anni. Sbagliò di 14' (I, *724*). [I am becoming a very serious man. Father used to say I would learn common sense at forty. He was fourteen years out.] Zeno, we recall, turned to commerce in the same year, and clearly the attitude of Cosini senior towards his son is based on that of Francesco Schmitz towards Ettore. But Svevo was not struck by his dying father; the death-bed blow is derived from an incident in the last illness of the mother of Svevo's painter-friend Veruda, whom I have already mentioned in relation to *Senilità*. Svevo has changed the sex of the parent and linked it to a possibly exaggerated version of his own father to form the climax of the fourth chapter and one of the central episodes of the novel.

One cannot therefore argue from the events of Svevo's fiction to those of his life on a one-for-one basis; and Svevo himself warned that the artist ought not to move in simplistic fashion directly from life to literature. In a note dated 2 December 1899, he stated that the best way to write seriously was to 'scribacchiare giornalmente'. Every day one should try to bring up an idea or feeling from the depths of one's being. 'Altrimenti facilmente si cade, – il giorno in cui si crede d'essere autorizzati di prender la penna – in luoghi comuni o si travia quel luogo proprio che non fu a sufficienza disaminato. Insomma fuori della penna non c'è salvezza' (III, *816*). [Scribble every day.

Otherwise, the day one thinks one has the right to take up the pen, one is likely to lapse into commonplaces, or corrupt that personal statement that was not examined carefully enough. In short, outside the pen there is no salvation.] It was of jottings of this kind that he wrote in December 1902: 'Io voglio soltanto attraverso a queste pagine arrivare a capirmi meglio' (III, *818*). [I simply want, by means of these pages, to reach a better understanding of myself.] But he added, in the 1899 note, that the daily jotting would never be anything more than 'la pagina più sincera di un'espressione troppo immediata e violenta' [a page of the utmost sincerity expressed in too immediate and violent a manner]. He recalls that Napoleon used to note things he wished to remember on pieces of paper which he then tore up, and he urges writers to follow that example: 'non permettete che questo primo immaturo guizzo di pensiero si fissi e incateni ogni suo futuro svolgimento' [Don't allow this first immature flash of thought to become fixed and obstruct its every future development]. In the light of these observations one can see the force – if not the precise target – of Svevo's criticism of *La coscienza di Zeno*, which was that there were one or two points at which he spoke his own thoughts through Zeno's mouth and the result was discordant.

Instead of asking what the novels and short stories tell us about the weakness of Ettore Schmitz, we should perhaps instead be asking what they tell us of the strength of Italo Svevo. Ettore Schmitz, the private citizen, is an elusive character. His wife has commented that he never revealed his doubts and disappointments to her, wishing instead that her life should be as untroubled as possible. In spite of the tenderness which his letters to her reveal, in spite of her respect for his vocation, her attempts to salvage his jottings and notes, and her devotion to his memory, one has the impression not merely that she did not understand him, but that he gave her little opportunity to understand him. If we now try to characterize Schmitz on the basis of his letters and diaries, we find that the portrait we draw bears only a faint resemblance to the image we have of Italo Svevo.

I mean by this that Italo Svevo is Ettore Schmitz's 'second self'; he is, as it were, a projection, for the duration of the story or novel, of those aspects of the author's personality which he values most highly for the purposes of that particular work. As W. C. Booth puts it in *The Rhetoric of Fiction*, the author, as he writes, 'creates not simply an ideal, impersonal "man in general" but an implied version of "himself" that is different from the implied authors we meet in other men's works. To some authors it has seemed, indeed, that they were discovering or creating themselves as they wrote.' One thinks here of Machiavelli's letter of 10 December 1513 to Francesco Vettori, in which he describes how, after a humdrum and even sordid day, in the evening he puts on fresh clothes, goes into his study and *becomes* what Booth would call his 'second self'. Or one thinks of Manzoni; rather a dull individual with neurotic tendencies, he becomes for a time the wise and witty narrator of *I promessi sposi*. In a similar way Schmitz becomes Svevo, into whom he projects qualities he admires, relegating to his characters those of his qualities of which he disapproves.

How then are we to characterize Svevo, the narrator of the first two novels and the guiding presence of the third, in which he has delegated his function as narrator to one of his characters? The answer is perhaps that although Svevo was using his fiction to project himself, or some of his personal problems, as well as to alleviate his intellectual loneliness, these were by no means his only, nor necessarily his most important, motives for writing. Indeed it is precisely because he does not wish primarily to project himself as an individual that he seeks to avoid intervening directly in the course of the narratives which he presents.

Svevo is one of the most lucidly intelligent of novelists. One of the most important of the operations in which he engages in his fiction is to allow his talent for demystification full scope and strip away his characters' illusions, exposing them for what they are and asserting the claims of reality. Nitti, in *Una vita*, is a provincial intellectual who tries to assert his cultural superiority and fails. His culture is second hand. We see him reading learned articles on the authenticity of some letters attributed to Petrarch, but we never see him reading Petrarch or responding imaginatively or creatively to anything. We do see him, however, prepared to sacrifice his taste, which is in reality rather better than that of the pretentious little salon in which he finds himself, to that of Annetta for the sake of his ambition and vanity. Worse still, we see that in his philosophizing, in which he wants to go beyond conventional morality, he is capable only of destructive, never of constructive, thought. The irresponsibility which makes him indulge in this kind of gesture eventually destroys him. On one level Svevo may have been attacking in Nitti something which he himself might have been, without the saving grace of irony; on another level he is dissecting one of the less edifying aspects of the cultural life of his time, the proliferation of provincial would-be supermen.

In that the plot of *Senilità* had its origin in Svevo's love affair with

Giuseppina Zergol, its inspiration is clearly autobiographical. Yet Brentani is only incidentally an aspect of Ettore Schmitz. He is, more importantly, a man of letters who is aware of the mediocrity of the novel he has written and tries to convert life into literature. Self-deception again causes havoc and misery, but one of the most important differences between this novel and *Una vita* is that whereas in the latter it was Nitti who paid the price of his own folly, in this novel Brentani escapes, not merely scot-free but into an altogether more comfortable cocoon of illusion. It is his sister who pays the toll inevitably exacted by life. Linked with this is another shift of emphasis in the second novel. *Una vita* was concerned with social structures and with the way in which two families, the Mallers and the Lanuccis, had in their different ways and at their different levels, reacted to the threat posed by the seduction of a daughter. The lower-class family purchase the seducer's favour by making it financially worth his while to marry Lucia; the Maller family, on the other hand, close ranks in order to keep the upstart Nitti out. *Senilità* lacks this social dimension, except in so far as Svevo draws attention to Brentani's financial circumstances and implies that in embarking on a facile love affair Brentani is merely doing what so many other young men about town are doing. There is, Svevo is telling us, nothing abnormal or socially unacceptable about Brentani's longing for facile pleasure. But Svevo focusses our attention more closely on Brentani than on the social pattern to which he is conforming because his concerns are not those of the sociologist. The enormity of his protagonist's behaviour on the moral plane is made all the clearer if he is deprived of a social alibi and we are shown the consequences of his behaviour for those about him. If the initial impulse behind a line of conduct which is to lead ultimately to Amalia's death is socially acceptable, so much the worse for society. Svevo is suggesting, however, that society is what men, by their individual choices, make it. These choices are always judged by Svevo in moral terms, and the lucidity with which he reveals his protagonists' shortcomings is always prompted by an ethical impulse.

To make a moral judgement of this kind implies that the individual in question is always free, within certain limits, to act differently if he makes the admittedly difficult effort to see the situation in its true light. Brentani need not have neglected his sister; Aghios could have helped Bacis; the 'buon vecchio' need not have 'purchased' the pretty girl. If one is conscious of the workings of the Schopenhauerian will, or the biological impulses of Darwinism, one can attempt to refrain from committing actions not in harmony with the ethical alternative with which Svevo proposes to replace the jungle morality of 'kill or be killed'. This is not withdrawal into pure contemplation in the manner of Schopenhauer; it is a loving and honest acceptance of one's fellow men, as the presence of the altruistic Elena Chierici in *Senilità* makes clear.

To say this is to make even clearer the basis of Svevo's condemnation of Zeno in *La coscienza di Zeno*, for what Zeno does is to succumb to 'war fever'; not, in his case, in militaristic form, but in Spencerian form. He does not fight in the war, but takes advantage of the abnormal conditions created by it to join in the social struggle. In his profiteering activities, Zeno makes his own the materialistic values of his society and opts for the easy kill in a jungle temporarily emptied of its fiercest predators. Svevo is careful to make it clear that the situation was not of his making and that his behaviour was not abnormal; weak-willed as he is, he merely succumbs to the pressure of circumstances and to his animal instincts. Yet the fact remains that he ought not to have done so. The light Svevo casts on the social, economic and cultural pressures acting on his protagonists ensures that we understand why they behave as they do, and how difficult it would be for them to behave otherwise, but in Svevo's austere world to understand all is not to forgive all. It is to ensure a proper basis for condemnation.

Does Svevo's condemnation of his character, Zeno, not imply a perhaps too harsh attitude towards himself, towards Schmitz the private citizen? The common factors of guilt and complicity in the war situation lead one to suggest that Schmitz's position was by no means the same as Zeno's and that Svevo, who was never overindulgent towards himself, has on this occasion judged himself too harshly. Zeno sacrifices his essential humanity when he becomes a war profiteer. He has to decide at that point to act, to join the competitive society. His only motive for doing so is the satisfaction he finds in victory. Schmitz, on the other hand, was involved in the war by virtue of the fact that he belonged to a successful and expanding company which was engaged in a primarily peaceful trade but which, because it manufactured an anti-fouling compound of unique efficacy, found itself being drawn into a trade which increasingly involved the navies of the main European powers. Svevo's dilemma was that if he were to adhere strictly to his socialist and pacifist principles he would have had to opt out of the business. But did he feel free to do so? In addition to the strong Jewish sense of the family bond, there was the question of his obligation to the employees. Perhaps he did not feel free to disengage himself from the situation. Moral gestures for which others pay the price are a form of self-indulgence. This is, in part, speculation, but *La coscienza di Zeno* suggests that Svevo was far from satisfied with his conduct.

The concluding paragraphs of the novel also suggest that Svevo, by the end of the war, had come near to despair. Implicit in *Senilità* is a faith in the power of the human mind to penetrate the layers of illusion with which human beings so frequently, and so frequently in vain, try to protect themselves from the demands of reality. A further implication in the novel is that the road to happiness can be discovered only by the mind, which is able to guide the impulses of the heart. But by the end of *La coscienza di Zeno*, in the final paragraphs of which Svevo surely speaks directly to us through the mouth of Zeno, mind itself is the enemy. Man's restless and inventive mind has been harnessed by his aggressive impulses. The rôles of mind and instinct have been reversed, and man is on the road to disaster. It is for this reason, and not on account of a fortuitous similarity between Zeno's prophecies of catastrophe and our nightmares of nuclear holocaust, that Svevo speaks so forcefully to a modern reader.

9. Language, Style and Techniques

Italy is a country in which literary traditions have been remarkably strong and in which successive generations of writers have had to come to terms with the 'questione della lingua' – the problem, that is, of what constitutes 'correct' literary usage. Italian as we know it in the masterpieces of Italian literature is in the main a written, literary, not a spoken, language, based on the usage of Tuscan authors, and purism, sternly hostile both to foreign loan-words and to dialectal elements from other parts of Italy, is a recurrent feature of literary debates from the Renaissance to the early decades of this century. Manzoni, a Lombard, came to terms with the problem by residing in Florence, revising *I promessi sposi* by purging it of all that was not pure Florentine, and republishing it in a definitive version in 1840. Verga attempted to solve it in his best novels and tales by fusing a more or less standard vocabulary with the speech rhythms and syntax of Sicilian in a style of unusual, but inimitable, vigour and efficacy – but which was nevertheless attacked by purists, for whom his innovations seemed too bold.

It was inevitable in these circumstances that Svevo should have been judged by his earliest Italian readers – and sometimes is still judged – according to linguistic criteria which to many modern Italian readers, and even more to non-Italians, appear unduly formalistic and even pedantic. C. Dionisotti has commented 'that *I Malavoglia* or *La coscienza di Zeno* needed rinsing in the Arno is an idea that occurred to no-one',[1] but even in 1926 and 1927, when long overdue recognition was finally accorded to him, it was being suggested that Svevo wrote in 'jargon', and that if he had followed Manzoni's example and polished his style there might have been some hope for him as a writer but now there was none. His success abroad has several times been 'explained away' by the statement that his style is such that it improves in translation. One naturally wonders what was the influence on criticisms of this kind of Crocean idealism. Croce's *Estetica* was published in 1902, and the linguistic discussions of the period between the two World Wars owe much to the vigour with which he propagated his ideas and the interest which they aroused among writers and critics. In so far as he insisted that the prime concern of the artist and critic should be with the expressiveness or otherwise of language, he was diverting attention away from such issues as grammatical correctness or non-Florentine usage and was urging linguistic liberalism. One can only conclude that in the 1920s either his influence was limited or the implications of his views were widely misunderstood. In any case, Crocean criticism, with its emphasis on poetic feeling, purity of style and harmony of form, was bound to be unsympathetic to a writer whose language is ungainly and unmusical.

Svevo was deeply sensitive to these criticisms of his style, some of which were voiced in the first reviews of *Una vita* and continued to be heard throughout his life, and he was greatly hurt by them. He was continually concerned about the issue of linguistic correctness, especially after he had become famous, when he felt under an obligation to give of his best every time he sat down to write. An English reader's natural reaction, with the benefit of hindsight, is to sympathize with Svevo and to feel impatience with his detractors: one would not after all dismiss Thomas Hardy out of hand because he makes mistakes in grammar and his diction is at times somewhat strained. Yet this is, in effect, one of the grounds on which Svevo has been rejected by many Italian critics, and not unnaturally. Writers from other parts of Italy had learned a literary form of Italian more successfully than he, and even his admirers have admitted that his style is defective, although they have been prepared to go on to argue that the blemishes were solely on the surface and were in any case redeemed by his good qualities. One must ask what there was in Svevo's style that so offended ears accustomed to more correct and more carefully cadenced prose, and why it was he never succeeded in eradicating his faults, if faults there are.

There are, in the first place, dialectal elements in his vocabulary, idiom and syntax. It has been suggested that Svevo would have written more correctly in German, but one has doubts about the truth of this statement. German, after all, was a language learned for the purposes of his education; his native language was Triestine, and it would have been natural for him to think, and for his characters to express themselves, in Triestine. But he could not write in dialect, partly because this would almost automatically have cut him off from the majority of his potential reading public, and partly because the choice of Italian, the national language, had political, anti-Austrian, overtones. (The desire to visit Florence was similarly motivated by political considerations, especially after the unification of

Italy, rather than by the need to absorb the language spoken there, which was not the literary language. There was of course the additional attraction that Florence was a lively cultural centre where several interesting literary movements were starting.) Svevo therefore transposes what he has to say into standard Italian. Inevitably traces of dialect remain in his lexicon. We find 'corame' for 'cuoio' (leather), 'servo di piazza' for 'facchino' (porter), 'coltrinaggi' for 'tende' (curtains), 'santolo' for 'padrino' (god-father), 'nettare' for 'pulire' (to clean), 'fabbricato' for 'edificio' (building), 'lastra' for 'finestra' (window, of both houses and cars). These examples are taken from the three novels and *La novella del buon vecchio e della bella fanciulla*, which shows that the dialectal substratum is a constant feature of Svevo's prose. One also finds dialectal idioms – 'fare la bella gamba' for 'to have a good time', 'stare a fitto' for 'to lodge', 'in lutto' instead of 'a lutto' for 'in mourning', 'gli avrebbe fatto male' instead of 'si sarebbe sentito male' for 'he would feel ill'. The regular use in unexpected situations of the preposition *di* is dialectal in origin, as in 'Non sarebbe stato meglio di renderla meno onesta e più astuta?' [wouldn't it be better to make her less honest and more cunning?] At times this usage resembles, and may be a product of, the German *zu*. In dialect this is rendered by *de*, which can mean both *di* and *da*.

The most thorough and detailed analysis of Svevo's language is that by Cernecca; but strangely the latter omits to draw attention in his lists of dialectal elements to the absence of words of Croat origin, which until recently were a striking feature of Triestine, as opposed to other Veneto dialects. The explanation would seem to be that the elimination of such words presented no great difficulty, and that the real difficulty for Svevo lay in the process of translating from dialect Italian into standard Italian. We may take the dialectal residue as evidence of incomplete success and of a certain strain involved in the process. It is interesting to find that Pirandello, whose Sicilian also differed radically from standard Italian, felt the same strain, at least initially, commenting in *L'umorismo* that a Tuscan writer such as Renato Fucini was fortunate that his language was so close to the literary norm. Pirandello dealt with the problems of language and dialect more successfully than Svevo, just as he dealt more successfully with the problem of presenting direct speech in standard Italian. There is no mistaking the confidently colloquial, 'spoken' tone and syntax of Pirandello's narrative prose and the nervous energy of his dialogue, which contrasts with Svevo's often very wooden dialogue, even in *La coscienza di Zeno*. 'Tullio mi disse: "spiegasti troppe cose ed io indovinai perciò che mentivi e che quella bella signorina era la tua amante" ' (II, ii, *803*). [You explained too much; I guessed at once that that charming young lady was your mistress.] What seems to have happened in cases like this, according to Devoto, is that Svevo conceived the passage initially in indirect speech – and in transposing it into direct speech changed the tenses to the past absolute instead of the more normal perfect tense. Tullio should surely have said '*Hai spiegato* troppo e perciò *ho indovinato*. ...'

The state of Svevo's manuscripts, with their frequent crossings-out, suggests that writing did not come easily to him. Cernecca suggests that Svevo mistrusted his dialect as a medium of expression and tried to avoid it, whereas his safest course would have been to make more extensive use of it. I am inclined to agree with the second part of that statement. In his letters Svevo refers to dialect with pleasure and affection – 'il mio caro veneto' (I, *255*) – and he was sensitively aware of Provençal dialect in Toulon. He uses Venetian effectively in direct speech in the tales *Cimutti* and *Marianno*, and Triestine for Carla's songs in *La coscienza di Zeno*. How much more effective would have been the episode in *Senilità* in which Balli insults Angiolina first in Italian and then in 'good Triestine' if we had been able to *hear* the transition. As Svevo says in the *Profilo autobiografico*: '... egli ben sapeva che la sua lingua non poteva adornarsi di parole ch'egli non sentiva. Non si può raccontare efficacemente che in una lingua viva e la sua lingua viva non poteva essere altra che la loquela triestina, la quale non ebbe bisogno di attendere il 1918 per essere sentita italiana' (III, *806*). [He was well aware that his language could not be embellished with words he did not feel. One can tell a story effectively only in a living language, and his living language could only be Triestine, which did not need to wait until 1918 to be felt as Italian.]

The attempt to use in his prose 'parole ch'egli non sentiva' may account for what Maier has described as 'hyper-correct forms' – 'salutifero' for 'salutare' (wholesome), 'ove' for 'dove' (where), 'dessa' for 'essa' (she), words with an excessively literary and archaic flavour which replace the more usual forms which are common to dialect and spoken Italian. Cernecca puts into this category the use of a plural in *ii* for nouns and adjectives ending in *io*, and the incorrect use of the subjunctive for the indicative ('Ho già capito di che si tratti'). Dialectal elements in the lexicon are no longer as offensive to Italian readers as they were in the early decades of this century, when critics tended to attach greater importance than they do now to the notion of linguistic purity. But inelegance and grammatical mistakes of the kind just mentioned, which disappear in translation, are still offensive, especially to those readers who expect prose narrative to be polished and carefully cadenced. One is bound to ask whether the clumsiness and grammatical incorrectness of Svevo's style are the result of a lack of sensitivity or skill on his part or whether they are in some way related to his aims and techniques.

Attempts are often made to illustrate Svevo's attitude to language and dialect by referring to a number of incidents in his novels. The first of these occurs in *Una vita*, in which Nitti is described as being 'afraid' of the work done by Miceni, whom he has to assist. Miceni is in charge of the Italian correspondence and the implication is that there is some linguistic weakness on Nitti's part, as there was on Svevo's. The other two incidents occur in *La coscienza di Zeno*. The first deals with Zeno's first encounter with Guido Speier; Zeno enviously notices that he speaks fluent Tuscan, while he and Ada are condemned to their 'wretched dialect'. The other occurs in the final section of the novel, when Zeno claims that no Triestine can ever write the truth in Tuscan and that his life would seem very different had it been described in dialect. These episodes may seem to confirm Cernecca's thesis that Svevo distrusted his dialect: but on the other hand one must remember that these episodes are intended primarily to tell us something about the characters in the novels, not about their author. Nitti has only a limited literary talent and little practical ability. Zeno envies Guido's poise, of which his ability to speak Tuscan is an element, but this poise turns out to be ill founded. The second reference to dialect in that novel is, as we have already seen, merely an excuse on Zeno's part and occurs in a passage distinguished by its comically bad logic. Why not quote, instead, that passage from *La novella del buon vecchio*, in which the narrator, describing the old man's attempts to write his thesis on the relations between the generations, states that many of his notes have to be thrown away because in them he had allowed himself to be distracted by the 'sound of the words' – 'si era lasciato deviare dal suono delle parole' (III, 65)? [he had let himself be led astray in them by the sound of the words.] The comment suggests that fine style can divert the attention from the sense, and we might more profitably approach the question of style from another direction. The corrections made to the second edition of *Senilità* are relevant to our discussion at this point.

The corrections are on the whole useful rather than outstandingly successful – apart from the excision of many superfluous exclamation marks and of an unnecessary passage on Brentani's dream-life. Some changes in vocabulary are acceptable because they conform to more normal usage – 'stupro' for 'violo' (rape), for example. Other changes eliminate useless archaisms – 'oriuolo' becomes 'orologio', for example. On the other hand other changes introduce more 'literary' and so less effective elements, as when Brentani is made to tell Balli that he had 'posseduto quella donna'. In 1898 he had simply 'had' her. The corrections in fact are curiously inconsistent. Wrong tenses remain, and subjunctives are changed to indicatives, indicatives to subjunctives, without apparent reason, *essere* and *avere* replace each other as auxiliary verbs according to no discernible pattern. Devoto concluded that the corrections were made in 'bad faith', without conviction. They were done at the request of the publisher, who wanted to present a more 'correct' text to his customers. It was, however, Cernecca who made the most startling discovery when he examined Svevo's copy of *Senilità*, on which the corrections had been made. They were in three different hands, and most of them were not the work of Svevo at all. He had been assisted by two friends. They presumably worked with him, or consulted him, but they did most of the work. Svevo, in other words, regarded changes of this kind as concessions to pedants and purists, and he effectively indicated his attitude when in the 1927 preface he stated that the novel was being republished with a few merely formal revisions.

This surprisingly dismissive comment, together with the reference to the danger of being seduced by the sound of the words, suggests that although Svevo was uncertain about some formal, grammatical aspects of the Italian language, he was not so much insensitive to the aesthetic qualities of prose as suspicious of them, regarding them as a distraction. Benco tells the story of how Svevo, as a reply to his critics, once wrote a page of good fourteenth-century prose to show how easily it could be done. The point is made obliquely in *Senilità*, in which there are several finely cadenced passages at key points in the narrative, usually followed by brusque deflationary statements intended to recall the reader to reality. This kind of technique can be used only by an author who is aware of the poetic possibilities of language but is willing to use them only for the purposes of irony because he suspects that his readers are liable to pay so much attention to the way in which he writes that they will fail to notice what he has to say. To this extent his style is, as Montale and others have remarked, 'anti-literary': he disliked 'la parola dolce ch'è tanto facile di vergare e che non dice niente'(I, *558*). [the harmonious phrase which is so easy to write but says nothing.] In the recurrent debate between the 'contenutisti' and the 'formalisti', between those who feel that content, and those who feel that form, is the prime consideration in a work of art, Svevo sides with the former, and his attitude anticipates that of M. Riffaterre, who in his *Essais de stylistique structurale* (1971) points out that a study of grammar and syntax tells one only about the author's grammar and syntax, not about his style. Since discussions of Svevo's style have so far concentrated on precisely these formal elements of language, much remains to be done before we can assess his style in the wider sense. I should, however, like to draw attention to three aspects of style: firstly, the description and presentation of characters; secondly, techniques of 'distancing'; and thirdly, the range and sources of Svevo's imagery.

We have already seen that the devices which Svevo uses in *Una vita* to present his excessively large gallery of minor characters are limited and liable to become monotonous. The narrative stops for a moment while we are given a brief account of the character in question in terms of one or two predictable physical characteristics – height, dress and, almost invariably, hair – and sometimes one or two psychological traits. The adjectives used are invariably generic. Lucia is 'magra, anemica ... bionda di un biondo tendente al rosso' (II, i, *145*). [Lucia was thin and anaemic ... with fair reddish colouring.] Sanneo is 'sulla trentina, alto e magro, i capelli di una biondezza sbiadita' (II, i, *136*) [about thirty, tall and thin, with light, faded hair]. The result is a series of identikit portraits which do not enable us to recognize anyone. The descriptions are uneconomical, using many words to little effect. We do not *need* all those details which seem to me to be merely the remains of a mimetic tradition which has outlived its usefulness. In *Senilità* the question of characterization is handled more confidently. There are fewer minor characters than in *Una vita*, and Svevo makes no attempt to tell us about their clothes and hair. Such details as we are given are all significant and acquire an almost emblematic value. Bardi is a spendthrift, Leardi a snob, Sorniani jaundiced and a malicious gossip: what more do we need to know?

One has the impression that the major characters are described in more detail, but as far as their physical attributes are concerned this is not really the case. Can one say what Brentani looks like in any detail? The accounts we are given of him concentrate on psychological analysis. Balli is presented as tall, bronzed and greying, with blue eyes and precisely pointed beard. The details confirm the hardness of his character. Angiolina and Amalia are described in a little more detail, mainly because we are able to see them through the eyes of both men. The former is 'una bionda dagli occhi azzurri grandi, alta e forte, ma snella e flessuosa' [a tall, healthy blonde, with big blue eyes and a supple, graceful body], as all can see, but when we see the effects of the light on her eyes, we are as much witnesses to Brentani's discovery that 'quell'occhio *crepitava*!' (II, i, *458–9*) [The light in her eye literally seemed to *crackle*!] as we are to the phenomenon itself. This technique is carried to its extreme conclusion in *La coscienza di Zeno*, in which descriptions of characters are always offered by another character, Zeno, and consequently are given in his words and tell us as much, if not more, about him than they do about those he describes. His account of Augusta, for example, is initially dismissive. He sees only her squint and so rules her out as a prospective bride; but later the squint becomes, as it were, less pronounced and his adjectives become less hostile, more affectionate, as he comes to appreciate her maternal qualities. His initial accounts of Carla, on the other hand, are significantly evasive: his adjectives this time are chosen so as to conceal those qualities which make him desire her. Hostility is the keynote of his account of Guido: hence details which in another man would have been completely innocuous – his ivory-handled walking-stick, his surprise when the table-turning episode apparently ceases to be a parlour game – all become in Zeno's emotionally coloured account opportunities to denigrate the dead man. This anticipates to some extent the question of the stylistic devices Svevo used to 'distance' himself from his characters, and at this point we must move to a discussion of some of Svevo's ironic strategies.

The narrator can make it clear that he does not wish to endorse his character's thoughts and attitudes by offering his own reflections on the narrative situation in generalized form in the present tense and by inserting such phrases as 'he thought', 'he felt' or 'it seemed to him' into the account he is giving of what was going on in his protagonist's mind. At times the statements thus made are immediately modified by the narrator: in the statement 'Alfonso credeva di avere dello spirito e ne aveva di fatto nei soliloqui' (II, i, *149*) [Alfonso considered himself to have poise. In his soliloquies he certainly had], the contrast between Nitti's interior monologues and his inept behaviour in society is made clear. At other times it is Nitti's actual behaviour, rather than any authorial comment, that modifies the statement, as when he goes for the first time to Maller's house: '"Venivo a disturbarla ..." e s'interruppe credendo di avere già espresso tutto il suo pensiero' (II, i, *152*). ['I was on my way to disturb you ...' and he interrupted himself, thinking he had already expressed all he wanted to say.] In reality he has said nothing, but this time the narrator prefers to show, rather than tell us.

The limitation of telling, as opposed to showing, is, from Svevo's point of view, that it draws attention to the presence of the narrator, and, from that of the reader, it is that the method is liable to become too mechanical. One finds Svevo using it with greater restraint in *Senilità*. It is, nevertheless, present at important moments, as when Brentani's 'experience' is first described as 'ciò ch'egli credeva di poter chiamare così' (II, i, *438*) [what he was pleased to call so], only to be redefined more accurately by the narrator. The account of Balli's aesthetic which follows is similarly, but discreetly, distanced. One notices that the account of the storm scene is punctuated by the observation that 'Ad Emilio parve che quel tramestío si confacesse al suo dolore' (II, i, *578*). [Emilio felt the confusion of the elements was attuned to his grief.] There is surely a world of difference, a far as the narrator's attitude is concerned, between that statement and the one which Svevo was careful not to make: 'Quel tramestío si confaceva al suo dolore'. [The confusion of the elements was attuned to his grief.]

There is one form of irony, however, which seems out of place in *Una vita* and is not to be found at all in *Senilità*. There are only perhaps a dozen examples of it in the whole novel: one or two will suffice here. Annetta is described by the narrator as 'trovando detti spiritosi o giudizî acuti che non avevano che il difetto di non trovarsi in buona armonia fra di loro' (II, i, *224*) [(finding) sharp or funny comments whose only defect was that they did not always suit the subject.] Nitti's philosophical treatise is described as foundering at the section in which 'non si trattava di annientare delle leggi ma di fabbricarne, cosa noiosissima' (II, i, *230*) [which did not deal with destroying, but creating laws, a very different and boring matter]. On these and similar occasions the narrator is indulging in a formal verbal irony which could well derive from Anatole France and at times betrays a certain intellectual arrogance which is not evident in his subsequent works. Although this method can give a measure of aesthetic satisfaction, more interesting, and more subtle effects are achieved by Svevo's use of indirect free style and of contrasts between illusion and reality to ironize his characters.

Language, Style and Techniques 117

In indirect free style the narrator presents his protagonist's thoughts and reactions without comment. He presents them in indirect speech, with verbs mainly in the imperfect or conditional, and usually in the words which his characters would have used in direct speech, and in the order in which they would have been spoken. In its simplest form indirect free style is rather like a series of statements on the pattern of 'He thought that ...' 'He felt that ...' with the introductory phrases omitted. This is a form of narration which Svevo finds congenial and he handles it with great skill. It is used, for example, in Nitti's first encounter with Annetta. Nitti is snubbed by her. 'Perché? Ella non lo aveva mai veduto prima di allora. Doveva essere semplicemente il disprezzo per l'inferiore, per la persona vestita male, perché ora egli sapeva quanto male egli fosse vestito' (II, i, *159*). [Why? She had never seen him before. It must all be contempt for an inferior, someone badly dressed; now he knew how badly dressed he was.] The question is Nitti's, as is the answer to it: the next sentence explains why Nitti arrived at that explanation. The narrator knows, as we learn later, that it is wrong: the truth is that one of Maller's employees had once paid court to Annetta and she had had to put up with a good deal of teasing from her father on the subject. She now treats his employees in this way in order to prevent a repetition of the incident. There is thus, even in *Una vita*, a series of shifts in the point of view from which the action is viewed, and Svevo's first novel is technically more complex than many critics have supposed. At times Nitti and Annetta are seen from the outside, by the narrator, who comments trenchantly on their behaviour, while sometimes Nitti is presented to us, without comment, on his own terms. The concluding paragraphs of chapter 20, in which we follow the mental processes which lead to Nitti's decision to commit suicide, are related almost entirely from his point of view; the implied reference to Schopenhauer exposes the fallacy in his argument. A clear hint that the narrator is presenting Nitti's point of view is given a few paragraphs earlier, when the reflections which follow his last conversation with Maller, presented in a form syntactically identical to the final paragraphs of the chapter, are described as a long soliloquy (II, i, *420*).

These shifts in point of view naturally occur more frequently in *Senilità*, which is in every way a more subtle and complex work. Phrases such as 'credeva', 'sentiva', by means of which the narrator explicitly dissociates himself from his protagonist occur less frequently than in *Una vita* – a fact which has given rise to the suggestion that Svevo adopts a more indulgent attitude towards Brentani. Of

Nitti, for example, he says: 'Egli s'era accorto della differenza che correva fra il suo modo di sentire e quello di coloro che lo contornavano e credeva consistesse nel prender lui con troppa serietà le cose della vita. Quella era la sua sventura!' (II, i, *244*). [He had noticed a difference between his way of feeling and that of the people around, and he thought this consisted in the fact that he took life too seriously. That was his misfortune.] In *Senilità* a similar reflection is presented differently. 'Come erano stati colpevoli lui e Amalia di prendere la vita tanto sul serio!' (II, i, *578*) [How wrong he and Amalia had been to take life so seriously!] In the first example it is the *credeva* that puts the reader on his guard: in the second, which is in indirect free style, Svevo relies on the reader's moral sense to warn him that it is monstrous that Brentani should compare his posturing to his sister's distress. Brentani has never taken life seriously enough.

There are in effect four points of view in *Senilità* – that of the narrator, who is often content to define, rather than to condemn explicitly, and that of three of the main characters, as we have already seen. Naturally the narrator's views tend to be made explicit more frequently in the early chapters, in which he is presenting his characters to the reader and setting up his 'experiment': when Svevo describes Brentani waiting impatiently for success 'come se l'età delle belle energie per lui non fosse tramontata' (II, i, *434*) [as if he had not already passed the age when his vitality was at the full], he reveals the vanity of Brentani's hopes. More frequently, however, he relies on a shift in point of view to cause doubts to rise in the reader's mind, especially as far as Angiolina and Balli are concerned. The former is not Brentani's *Ange*, but neither, we suspect, is she Balli's *Giolona*: the sculptor's characterization is too simplistic to be acceptable. Balli himself we see through the admiring eyes of the other three characters, but inevitably we are compelled to ask ourselves whether their admiration, in view of his failure as an artist and his insensitivity as a human being, is not really the expression of some weakness in their characters, the result of something which they lack, rather than a just tribute to his excellence. Thus the narrator is able to avoid altogether the formal verbal irony which at times gave *Una vita* so arrogant a tone and, more importantly, he avoids seeming to impose his judgement of his characters on the reader. They stand condemned by virtue of what they are and do, or fail to be and do, not by virtue of a moral code imposed on them from above. Few novelists have used the shifting point of view so consistently, or to such good effect.

LANGUAGE, STYLE AND TECHNIQUES   119

In both *Una vita* and *Senilità* much use is made of what is usually termed the Irony of Events, which is, technically, one of the most interesting features of *Una vita*. Thus Nitti abandons Annetta's *salon*, making an iron resolution to devote himself to work, only to return to her without waiting to be asked. Later, when he has made little progress with her, he resolves to treat her coldly, but is totally incapable of doing so. He dreams of becoming indispensable at the bank – only for the death of Jassy, who had thought himself indispensable, to leave the bank totally unaffected in a way which anticipates the indifference to Nitti's death implied in the final letter. He thinks he has achieved detachment, only to find himself squeezing the last drop of gratification from his generosity to Lucia. A pattern of behaviour is thus established and we are conditioned to expect his final gesture to be a failure.

This discrepancy between declared intentions and actual conduct is a major source of irony in *Senilità*. Brentani's resolutions to treat his love affair as a source of facile pleasure, his resolve to dedicate himself to his sister, his determination to part from Angiolina with calm and dignity – all are condemned in advance to end in failure. In a sense, therefore, there is in both novels a progressive slackening of the dramatic tension: then how is it that both novels retain an element of tension? The reason seems to be that there is always one character, the protagonist, who fails to discern the emergent pattern. His failure to analyse himself is such that each new turn of the screw is the source in him of painful surprise; each new discovery of weakness is to him revelation which confirms in the reader's mind the condemnation prompted by Svevo's use of a changing point of view.

The first two novels, written within a few years of each other, naturally have much in common in spite of the greater maturity of the second. *La coscienza di Zeno*, on the other hand, was written much later. Since the unreliable Zeno tells his own story it uses a narrative technique which at first seems radically different from that of the first two novels. Svevo now relies entirely on showing, rather than telling, and indirect free style is abandoned in favour of a 'direct' free style which enables Zeno to relate the events of his life from the point of view of 1914 and 1915–16. The differences, however, are less notable than they seem and the novelty of the psychoanalytic situation conceals techniques which are tried and tested. We have no difficulty in seeing that Zeno's capacity for ironizing at his own expense resembles that of Nitti and Brentani, or that the Irony of Events, whereby Zeno marries the wrong girl, who turns out to be the right one after all, and wins his way to wealth and success, is but the comic version of the Irony of Events which Svevo had used previously to achieve such sombre effects. And by making Zeno tell his own story Svevo makes use of what is usually termed the Irony of Self-revelation in a form so consistent and extended that many have failed to recognize it. Yet surprise is as constant a feature of *La coscienza di Zeno* as it is of the other novels. 'Sorpresa' and 'meraviglia' are recurrent features of Svevo's vocabulary, and Zeno's discovery that life is original is not a measure of his philosophical understanding in existentialist vein, but of his failure to understand himself.

Certain features of Svevo's imagery are almost as constant in his work as are his ironic strategies. Their sources are fields as diverse as those of music, the visual arts, business and commerce, social philosophy, Darwinism and the animal world. All these were areas in which he was keenly interested throughout his life and in which he never ceased to pursue new ideas and experiences. The presence in his novels of imagery derived from all these sources is an indication of the way in which he tried constantly to synthesize these apparently disparate interests into a coherent whole and relate them to his art. Svevo's imagery is neither decorative nor ostentatious, but always functional, always reinforcing the message of the novels.

Metaphors derived from the concept of the 'struggle for life' as developed by Spencer constitute one of the most regularly recurring forms of imagery in Svevo's novels. We have already seen that Nitti's Trieste is a battlefield and that the language of social Darwinism recurs at key moments in *La coscienza di Zeno*; one could in fact find fault with *Una vita* on the grounds that such imagery occurs too frequently, thus creating the impression that Svevo's imagery is more limited than in fact it is. Images of battle occur rather less frequently in *Senilità* than in *Una vita*, and they are used in the second novel with more skill, as in the first part of chapter v, in which the rivalry of Balli and Brentani for the attention of Amalia is described consistently in terms of struggle in a metaphor which is sustained for five pages.

The impression of stylistic poverty created by the excessive use in *Una vita* of one form of imagery is misleading since Svevo also makes interesting and effective use of imagery derived from the visual arts. This form of imagery is commonly associated with *Senilità*, in which one of the characters is a sculptor and in which the two main female characters are described in terms of colour, and skilful evocations of landscape are used ironically. It is usual to attribute this aspect of

Language, Style and Techniques

Senilità to the influence of Veruda, who no doubt did much to deepen Svevo's understanding of the arts – a debt which the novelist acknowledged in his later fiction. But other novelists in whom Svevo was interested – Stendhal, Zola, the Goncourt brothers – were also interested in painting, and the friendship with Veruda began because Svevo already had an interest in the arts. Nitti knows little about the arts, but the narrator of *Una vita* has a fine eye for painterly effects. The bare corridor of the bank, in which Nitti spends so many bleak hours, is compared to a study in perspective; a landscape under a cloudless sky is made to reflect Nitti's state of mind by being compared to an oleograph in which the painter's shades of colour have been made uniform by mechanical reproduction. Nor should one forget the rich colours of the Maller home, contrasting with those of the bank. Santo emerges from a kitchen in which copper vessels gleam in the light as in a Dutch genre painting: one feels at that point that Nitti would be more at home in the servants' quarters. And it is in the Maller house that Nitti sees an important painting – a rocky Carso landscape which has a dual rôle in that it both points to the present bleakness of his life and hints at the falsity of his Arcadian ideal.

Images deriving from music are to be found less frequently than those based on the visual arts, but music nevertheless plays an important part in Svevo's fiction. It is music that reveals to Nitti his need to hear a friendly voice, while Brentani's moments of harmony with Angiolina can be described as music interrupted by the inevitable discords of her tactlessness. A lesser Venetian canal can be seen in relation to the Grand Canal in *Corto viaggio sentimentale* as a 'rio dove le forme grandiose del canale si riducevano e variavano in motivi capricciosi ch'erano la continuazione, anzi, la integrazione della forte armonia che non ancora aveva liberato i loro sensi' (III, *192–3*) [*rio*, where the stupendous forms of the canal were reduced in scale and ran to capricious variations – the continuation, and integration, of the grand melody still resounding in their ears]. But it is in *La coscienza di Zeno* that music comes into its own as an element of plot and structure. Carla sings in two styles: her first attempts at opera conceal her true talent, which is for a more intimate and subdued style. Guido and Zeno both play the violin in a way which is a comment on their character. Guido is unable to be true to the music he plays and vulgarizes it; Zeno lacks poise and harmony but has more real feeling than his rival. And Zeno regularly describes relationships in musical terms of discord and harmony. In all these cases the meaning of an incident or episode is reinforced by an image without any explicit intervention or comment on the part of the author.

One is not surprised to find Svevo using in his imagery the language of the commerce on which Trieste's wealth was founded and in which so many of his characters are engaged. Liquidation is a startling metaphor for death (I, 506), but in general Svevo uses business imagery for two purposes. It can illustrate the ways in which relationships have been devalued by the 'cash ethic'. Brentani cynically describes 'respectable women' as those who have found a purchaser prepared to pay the right price – which is presumably marriage, viewed as a business contract, whereas he merely gives Angiolina money without realizing the implications of what he is doing. And the 'buon vecchio' sees the pretty girl merely as an object to be bought if she is for sale. Perhaps she has no name because she is treated as an object and not a person. The second use of this kind of imagery is for comic effect, as when someone acknowledges receipt of a slap or a pinch, or when Zeno describes his daughter as 'una piccola balla di merci che aveva bisogno dello speditore per muoversi' (III, 396) [a little bale of merchandise that could not move without a shipping agent] since she has to be accompanied when she goes out. Irony of this kind is two-edged, however; it may show the character described in a comic light, but it also makes one wonder what values are held by the narrator. Zeno's choice of language on these occasions is very revealing.

It is equally natural that Svevo, who had read a good deal of Darwin and was an inveterate zoo-visitor, should make extensive use of animal imagery. There is little about his use of such imagery in *Una vita,* however, that is unusual, except in the way in which Macario uses the seagulls to explain his view of society to Nitti and offers a biological explanation of the latter's failure to adapt. Nor is the imagery of *Senilità* any more remarkable in this respect. The consistently ironic use of animal imagery is a late development and is to be found first in tales such as *Orazio Cima, Il malocchio* and *La buonissima madre*. There is no naïve extrapolation on Svevo's part from animal to human behaviour; animal images are simply part of the ironist's equipment, a Darwinian variation on the older techniques whereby people are made comic by being described as things or machines. Zeno naturally makes frequent use of comparisons which have this intention. His description of Augusta's youngest sister as a little viper is conventional abuse, but his account of himself, disappointed in his desire for Felicita, is richly comic: 'Io in quel momento ero avviato all'amore e proprio alla mia età si somiglia molto al coccodrillo in terra ferma di cui si dice che abbisogni di tanto tempo per mutare di direzione ...' (III, 451). [At the moment I was bent on love, and at my age, one is rather like a crocodile on dry land – it takes a long time to change direction.] At other times, as when he compares Augusta to a swallow or an ant, there are, in view of the philosophy on which the novel is based, overtones of which it is hard to believe that Zeno is aware, in spite of the final paragraphs of *La coscienza di Zeno*.

The form in which evolution was popularized was 'man is descended from the monkeys'. This explains not only Svevo's use of animal imagery as discussed so far, but also why, when Zeno begins to take an interest in induced rejuvenation, he is concerned particularly with the method advocated by Serge Voronoff (1866–1951). It was widely assumed that the ageing process was caused by the loss of sexual power, rather than the former being the cause of the latter. Surgeons set most store on vasectomy and vasco-ligature (the Steinach operation undergone by W. B. Yeats in 1934), but the layman commonly associated rejuvenation with animal experiments. C. E. Brown-Sequard injected himself with testicular material from dogs and guinea-pigs, and Voronoff specialized in the transplantation of testicular tissue from monkeys to humans. Brown-Sequard's dogs are perhaps the cause of the recurrent dog imagery in Svevo's later work, notably in *Corto viaggio sentimentale*. In *Il mio ozio*, and even more in *La rigenerazione*, Svevo – figuratively speaking – makes a monkey out of Zeno Cosini and Giovanni Chierici. Zeno speculates about the effect of the operation: will the elderly patient climb a tree when he sees a beautiful woman? Thus sexual desire brings out the animal in man, in one way or another, and the whole question of the rejuvenation operation, which Zeno never gets as far as describing, emerges as an extended animal image, which Svevo exploits for the possibilities of irony which it offers.

Given the present state of Svevo studies, the conclusions which emerge from a survey of this kind will inevitably be tentative, since this is an area in which much work remains to be done. It must be admitted that Svevo's style is inelegant and has shortcomings on the formal level. On the other hand it must also be recognized that on the intellectual level it is more subtle and richer in imagery than has generally been supposed. Sustained irony demands precision and intellectual clarity rather than lyrical effusion. These are qualities which Svevo has in good measure. The reader is, moreover, often surprised by the overtones of his imagery, which are liable to escape those who are not aware of the extent of his culture. His youthful ideal was that an author's works should enable one to see how a cultured contemporary saw life. It was clearly one which he endeavoured consistently to live up to. Thus his language and style are functional, not decorative: their appeal is intellectual, not musical or sensual. They are the tools of an ironist.

10. Italo-German Novelist : a Perspective

Widely differing interpretations have been offered of Svevo's work. For some he is a true Romantic, projecting himself in his heroes and sympathizing with them; for others he is a Decadent, believing in nothing and dissolving all creeds in the acid of his irony; for others still he is an impassioned Marxist critic, exposing the inner contradictions of bourgeois society. Is competition, with the consequent corruption of all moral values, seen by Svevo as the result of certain social structures, or are the latter themselves the result of man's aggressive impulses? This debate, like that on the question as to whether Zeno is cured, and if so, of what, is likely to continue for some time yet.

Svevo has, moreover, been compared to a number of widely, almost bewilderingly, different novelists, including Proust, Kafka, Joyce, Mann and Musil. Critics in search of his sources claim to have discovered them in novelists as diverse as Tolstoy, Dostoevsky, Stendhal, Flaubert and Zola. His influence has been growing in recent years, and in his own country he has helped to shape the careers of Moravia, Berto and Buzzati. In France he has been held up for admiration by Robbe-Grillet. In the United States he has exercised a remarkably strong influence over Norman Mailer, Phillip Roth and Saul Bellow. In England he is admired by Melvyn Bragg and imitated by David Storey.

One may feel that the novelists to whom he has been compared, or whom it is suggested that he has influenced, have little in common. This is true, but to say so is not to provide evidence of disastrous disarray in the ranks of the Svevo scholars and critics. There have in fact been considerable advances in Svevo studies in recent years. It is, rather, evidence of Svevo's essential complexity. To present an over-simplified account of him would be to do him a grave disservice.

At the same time one cannot help noticing that the novelists whose influence is central to his development – Stendhal and Flaubert – are, naturally, ironists, as are two of those to whom he has most profitably been compared, namely Mann and Musil.

At this point Svevo's Italo-German pseudonym and his education in Germany assume a new significance. German names have been cited frequently in the course of this study. Svevo's German was fluent. He admired Goethe and Schiller. He read widely in German philosophy. German gave him access to Darwinism and to the work of Freud, long before the latter became known in Italian. He read Shakespeare and the Russian novelists in German. His cultural background has much in common with that of Mann and Musil. For much of his life he was, like the latter, an Austrian subject: his interest in the unconscious, like the former's, was shaped by Schopenhauer and Freud. His irony in fact belongs to the same tradition as that of Mann and Musil.

Their tradition is that of German Romantic Irony. 'Romantic' may seem a strange epithet to apply to the lucidly intelligent Svevo, much of whose irony is directed to attacking the neo-romantic, anti-rational cult of energy and action. Paradoxical though the label may seem, one has to use it since there was a time-lag of over a century between the formulation of the theories on which it is based and the writing of literature which put them into practice.

The theories were formulated in Germany in the late eighteenth and early nineteenth centuries, mainly by Friedrich von Schlegel (1772–1829) and his brother August (1767–1845), the brilliant translator of Shakespeare, and Jean-Paul Richter (1763–1825). They saw irony as a means of achieving several aims. It enabled the artist both to be present in his work and simultaneously to indicate his detachment from it, both to express himself and also to distance the self which expresses from the self which is expressed. Petrarch is cited by August Schlegel as a poet who has Romantic Irony in that he smiles at his own sentimentality. This use of irony must have appealed to Svevo as a means of exorcizing personal inadequacies or 'unhealthy' tendencies in his psychological make-up. Irony is also seen as a means of recognizing the essentially paradoxical nature of the world; an ambivalent, ironic attitude is seen as the only way in which the basic contradictions of life can be expressed but not resolved, since to resolve them would be to fall into the kind of over-simplification the ironist often attacks. Irony is seen, finally, as a means of dealing with the contradictions of art which depicts life, and is not itself life but which, nevertheless, makes the same claims to verisimilitude as life. Paintings of three-dimensional scenes exist in two dimensions only: novels depict the flux of life, and in so doing, fix it, so that it ceases to be flux. Romantic Irony makes explicit the paradoxes which lie behind the conventions we normally accept without question.

Romantic Irony in Germany was originally more a matter of literary theory, of a programme for literature, than literature itself. The theorists saw in Romanticism the seeds of the modern. Jean-Paul, Heine and E.T.A.Hoffmann only partially put the theories into practice and it is only with the novels of Thomas Mann that one finds the best, most thorough-going examples of Romantic Irony in practice, over a century after the theories were formulated. One can see Musil, too, as a Romantic Ironist.

The links in the chain connecting Svevo to this German tradition are to some extent a matter of conjecture at present and are likely to prove a fruitful field of research in the future. I cannot demonstrate that he had read Friedrich Schlegel, but I think it very likely that he did. He must have read Shakespeare in August's translation, and probably also a certain amount of German Shakespeare criticism. He certainly read Heine on Shakespeare, who looms large in all theoretical discussions of irony at this time. We know that he read many of the works of both Heine and Jean-Paul. It is also interesting to see the way in which the name of Musil occurs regularly in Maxia's *Lettura di Svevo* as a useful term of comparison, and L.R.Furst has profitably compared *La coscienza di Zeno* and Mann's *The Magic Mountain*, which was published less than a year after Svevo's novel and deals with remarkably similar themes. I would also suggest that Jacob's cry in *Joseph and his Brothers* – 'How shall a man live if he cannot rely on things turning out differently from what he thought?' – neatly encapsulates a very Svevian paradox. Thus Svevo, whose first novel appeared in 1892, is a precursor of both Mann and Musil. The former's *Buddenbrooks*, which was begun in 1897 and published in 1900, is as Schopenhauerian as *Una vita* and deals, like *Senilità*, with the conflict between art and life. Part of Musil's *Man without Qualities* was written at the same time as Svevo's *La coscienza di Zeno*, but was not published until 1930–43. All three novelists attempt to diagnose the ills of their society in similar terms. This is not to suggest that Svevo influenced the course of the German novel, since there is no reason to suppose that the Germans knew of his work, although it seems that he read Mann: it is rather a question of shared influences producing, independently, similar results in different countries. There is a parallel here with the Svevo-Pirandello relationship. Svevo constantly anticipates the latter's themes of rôle-playing, the relativism of truth and the attempt to superimpose art on life. Again there is little question of Svevo influencing Pirandello – who was also educated in Germany, at Bonn – but it is difficult, when dealing with the subsequent development of these themes in Italian literature, to disentangle the influence of Svevo from that of Pirandello.

The humour of *La coscienza di Zeno* has led to a perhaps excessive emphasis on the dissolving effect of Svevo's irony, to the assumption that he, like Zeno in old age, takes nothing seriously and uses humour as a means of avoiding commitment to any positive human values. It is true that even as a young man Zeno could say of the table-turning episode that he wanted only to laugh and that he expected no-one to take the matter seriously. The whole episode contrasts strikingly with the horrifying appearance of the dead Joachim in *The Magic Mountain*, just as Zeno's pleasurable profiteering contrasts with our final glimpse of Hans Castorp as a soldier in the 1914–18 war. For this reason I cannot accept the view, put forward most recently by Furbank, that *Zeno's* humour and irony constitute a 'positive' or 'healthy' response on *Svevo's* part to life's horrors. Zeno's humour is irresponsible, and his jokes are not Svevo's. Svevo never jokes about serious issues; egoism, cruelty and war are not for him a source of humour. His irony does indeed have a corrosive effect, but on illusions rather than ideals, and it is always used with a remarkable sense of responsibility. His antipathies always imply his sympathies: if he exposes irresponsibility, egoism and self-deception, it is because he believes in the value of clarity and love. He is above all a moralist who would like to believe in man's freedom to make ethical choices but sees human nature – and consequently society – as being irremediably flawed by conflicting impulses towards good and evil. Since this is so he cannot place his faith in any of the creeds or systems which the science and philosophy of his time offer as universal panaceas for the ills from which either individuals or society suffer. How can he in honesty believe in a cure for the incurable, a solution to the insoluble? Irony does indeed, in this sense, denote non-commitment, but it is perhaps the only alternative to despair.

Here one is faced with questions which are perhaps insoluble. Is Svevo's view of human nature equivalent to the doctrine of Original Sin, a residue of his religious upbringing and another manifestation of the burden of Jewishness? Is it the result of an inability to synthesize into a coherent system the ideas and perceptions he had derived from his reading and his experience? Or did he consciously decide that life was a tangled web of unresolvable contradictions? The essay 'Un individualista' and the novel *Una vita* seem to imply that men are to a great extent moulded – or distorted – by society. To go on then to ask who or what moulds society is to engage in an inconclusive circular argument. *Senilità* and the later fiction, on the other hand, seem to imply that the Marxist critique of society is an over-simplification and that there is an unresolved conflict in human nature. Man may know the direction in which he wishes to develop, but Svevo's men are unable to take Spencer's advice and control their own evolution, which will always be directed by the unpredictable impulses of the spirit, and these are all too often directed, whether by animal instincts or by the scheming mind, to evil ends.

This is perhaps why Svevo rarely uses Romantic Irony as a means of dealing with the ironic contradictions of art as fully as Mann does. The latter's Joseph knows that he is a character in a story, and reminds both his brothers and Mut that this is the case. Brentani does indeed act out the novel he cannot write and subsequently fails to turn his adventure into fiction, but he does not formulate the concepts involved in explicit terms for the benefit of other, less aware characters in the novel; nor does he know that he is acting out his novel within another novel, of which he is not the author – unless, that is, one accepts the rather improbable hypothesis that the narrator of *Senilità* is Brentani, telling his own story in the third person singular. Nor does Zeno remind us of his own complex situation as a character within a fiction of his own devising within a fiction which is not of his devising. And only occasionally, in his correspondence, do Svevo's references to contracts and to literature as a product sound like a Triestine businessman's ironic version of the artist as god-like creator. On the whole Svevo uses Romantic Irony to offer a critique of life rather than of art.

In order to do so he makes use of philosophies and scientific discoveries which challenge generally accepted notions of the established order of things, such as Darwinism, Marxism and Freudianism. He never uses them in such a way as to suggest that he merely wishes to replace one orthodoxy with another, but rather to question the adequacy of any orthodoxy to embrace the complexities of life, to which he wishes his art to be true.

It is one of the ironies of the history of Svevo's reputation that the characteristics which distinguished him as an ironist and as an innovator and led some English and French readers to recognize his merits at a time when he was still little known in Italy, have subsequently led to his being overshadowed by the recognition given to German and, to some extent to American, novelists. In part the reason for this is that the witty paradoxes of Mann and Musil are more accessible than the discreet hints of Svevo; Mann's earnestness, in particular, is less disconcerting than Zeno's humour. In part, however, the reason is that Svevo lacks Mann's imaginative ability to re-create with great vividness a historical setting remote in every way from that in which we live. Mann ranges impressively from Goethe's Weimar to Joseph's Egypt. Svevo never re-creates historical settings. He rarely moves geographically beyond Trieste, and then only as far as Venice or some other northern Italian town, and he prefers to deal with certain regularly recurring types of character. This may be the inevitable result of his use of literature as therapy, or of his continual preoccupation with the problems of the society in which he lived, but although his range is restricted in this sense he raises issues of general concern and within his self-imposed limits he achieves a remarkable excellence.

For this reason it is disappointing to find that there has grown up over the years in the reading public something like an unspoken or unwritten assumption – none the less powerful for not being articulated – that Svevo is a novelist's novelist, just as it used thoughtlessly to be said that Spenser was a poet's poet. The implication is that he is of interest only to practitioners of the craft of novel-writing. I would suggest that far from creating a barrier between Svevo and a wider audience, the interest which other writers have taken in him – an interest which has been increasing in recent years – should constitute an incentive to the curious reader anxious to extend the range of his experience. If so many, and so different, novelists have found so much to admire and imitate in Svevo, cannot this much, which is far from consisting solely of 'tricks of the trade', be a source for others of pleasure and enrichment? And if it is at the same time disturbing and challenging, is that not something to be grateful for at a time when so much that is offered for our consumption is merely anodyne? For Svevo is a major novelist in the mainstream of the European tradition. The culture in terms of which he expresses himself is for most part as alive now as when he wrote – witness current trends in ethology and anthropology; his concerns – man's egoism and brutality, his capacity for self-deception and for hope, the problem of aggression in a competitive society and the ethical alternatives to it, the potential of the mind for good and for evil – are still ours and are likely to remain so for a long time to come. In a world in which irrationalism and anti-intellectualism are endemic diseases, Svevo's intelligent irony speaks with the voice of health.

Notes

Chapter One: Essays and Explorations
1. C. Bermant, *The Cousinhood* (London 1971) 192
2. U. Saba, *Storia e cronistoria del 'Canzoniere'*, in *Prose*, a cura di L. Saba (Milan 1964) 407.
3. Most of Svevo's essays are published in *Opera omnia*, vol. III. For 'Critica negativa', see *Umana*, January 1972, pp. 12–15.
   For the remainder, see B. Moloney, 'Italo Svevo e *L'Indipendente* sei articoli sconosciuti' (to be published shortly in *Lettere italiane*).

Chapter Two: Plays
1. L. Veneziani Svevo, *Vita di mio marito* (Trieste 1958) 51.
2. For the dating of the plays I have modified the chronology suggested by B. Maier, 'Il teatro di Italo Svevo e la proposta di un'altra data per *L'avventura di Maria*', in *Il Dramma*, XLV (1969) 4, 26–9, and G. Rustia, *Il teatro di Italo Svevo. Proposte per una cronologia e per un' edizione critica*. Tesi di laurea, Università degli Studi di Trieste, Facoltà di Lettere e Filosofia, Anno accademico 1969–70, a copy of which is in the Svevo collection in the Biblioteca Civica of Trieste.
3. The text of *Ariosto Governatore* will be found in G. Spagnoletti, 'La giovinezza e la formazione letteraria di Italo Svevo' in *Studi Urbinati* 27 (1973) 1–2, 179–221.
4. It contains a reference to J. Lubbock's *Ants, Bees, Wasps* (1882), which came out in German translation in 1883, which rules out an earlier date.
5. The undated typescript is signed 'Italo Svevo', which establishes the *terminus a quo*, and linguistic evidence – e.g., *volontieri* for *volentieri* – the *terminus ad quem*.
6. Apollonio assigns it to 1880, but the action takes place in 1913–14.
7. Assigned by Apollonio to 1880, it refers to Trieste's Via Corsi, so called only from 1921. Rustia's analysis of the language provides the *terminus ad quem*. This play is signed, unusually, 'E. Muranese', which suggests that it may have been written while Svevo was working at the Veneziani factory at Murano.
8. Quoted by A. Momo, 'Il teatro di Italo Svevo' in *Ateneo Veneto* 5 (1967) 107–31, p. 126

Chapter Three: First Narrative Fiction
1. It was published by F. Carlini in *Paragone* 30 (1972) 264, 61–72, after attention had been drawn to it by R. Rimini, 'Due scritti del giovane Svevo', in *Belfagor* 26 (1971) 5, 599–600.
2. A. Schopenhauer, *The World as Will and Representation*, translated by E. F. J. Payne, 2 vols (New York 1969) vol. I, p. 398.

Chapter Four: *Senilità*
1. D. J. Enright, 'Svevo's Progress: or, The Apotheosis of the Poor Fish', in *Conspirators and Poets* (London 1966) 167–75.
2. P. Spriano, *Socialismo e classe operaia a Torino dal 1892 al 1913* (Turin 1958).

CHAPTER SIX: *La coscienza di Zeno*
1. 'Recommendations to Physicians practising Psycho-analysis', in *The Complete Psychological Works of Freud*, vol. 12 (London 1958) 111–12.
2. See, for examples, W.C. Booth, *The Rhetoric of Fiction* (Chicago and London 1969) 372–4.
3. Definitions of psychological terms are taken from H.B. and A.C. English, *A Comprehensive Dictionary of Psychological and Psycho-analytical Terms: A Guide to Usage* (New York/London/Toronto 1958).
4. L.N. Tolstoy, *Anna Karenin*, translated and with an introduction by Rosemary Edmonds (Penguin Books 1971) 278.
5. R.R. Wisse, *The Schlemiel as Modern Hero* (Chicago and London 1972) 90.

CHAPTER SEVEN: Last Narrative Fiction
1. See J.-N. Schifano, 'Esquisse pour une psychobiographie d'Italo Svevo', in *Italica* 48 (1971) 4, 25–45.

CHAPTER EIGHT: Autobiography and Art
1. See especially D. Fernandez, *L'Arbre jusqu'aux racines* (Paris 1971); and for an application of the method to Svevo see J.-N. Schifano, 'Esquisse pour une psychobiographie d'Italo Svevo', cit.

CHAPTER NINE: Language, Style and Techniques
1. Quoted in B. Migliorini, *The Italian Language*, abridged and recast by T. Gwynfor Griffith (London 1966) 470. For a useful statement of Professor Griffith's views on Svevo's language, see his review of Furbank, op. cit., in *Critical Quarterly* 10 (1968) 3, 300–2.

Select Bibliography

General Note

The *Opera omnia*, published by Dall'Oglio, Milan, consists of the following volumes:

I. *Epistolario*, premessa di Letizia Svevo-Fonda Savio, introduzione e note di Bruno Maier (1966)
II. *Romanzi*, introduzione e bibliografia di Bruno Maier (1969). (Part I contains a lengthy introduction, the texts of *Una vita* and the 1927 edition of *Senilità*; part II contains *La coscienza di Zeno*, the 1898 version of *Senilità*, and a bibliography.)
III. *Racconti – Saggi – Pagine sparse*, a cura di Bruno Maier (1968)
IV. *Commedie*, introduzione e note di U. Apollonio (1969)

Translations of quotations, with a few exceptions, are from the Uniform Edition, published by Secker and Warburg. The Uniform Edition consists of the following volumes:

I. *Confessions of Zeno*, translated from the Italian by Beryl De Zoete, with a Note on Svevo by Eduardo Roditi (1962)
II. *As A Man Grows Older*, translated from the Italian by Beryl De Zoete (1962)
III. *A Life*, translated from the Italian by Archibald Colquhoun (1963)
IV. *Short Sentimental Journey and other stories*, translated from the Italian by Beryl De Zoete, L. Collison-Morley and Ben Johnson (1967)
V. *Further Confessions of Zeno*, translated from the Italian by Ben Johnson and P.N. Furbank (1969)

The best biography of Svevo is P.N. Furbank's *Italo Svevo. The Man and the Writer* (London, Secker and Warburg, 1966) but see also L. Veneziani Svevo, *Vita di mio marito*, 2nd ed. (Trieste, Edizioni dello Zibaldone (1968).

Other important monographs on Svevo are: A. Leone De Castris, *Italo Svevo* (Pisa, Nistri-Lischi, 1959); M. Forti, *Svevo romanziere* (Milan, All'insegna del Pesce d'oro, 1966); N. Jonard, *Italo Svevo et la crise de la bourgeoisie européenne* (Paris, Société des Belles-Lettres, 1969); G. Luti, *Italo Svevo e altri studi sulla letteratura italiana del primo Novecento* (Milan, Lerici, 1961); B. Maier, *Italo Svevo*, 2nd ed. (Milan, Mursia, 1968); S. Maxia, *Lettura di Italo Svevo* (Padova, Liviana, 1965).

The best (but incomplete) Svevo bibliography is that compiled by B. Maier in Svevo, *Opera Omnia*, vol. II, ii, pp. 1105–1228. This omits much criticism in English, for which see S. Pacifici, 'Italo Svevo's antiheroes', in *The Modern Italian Novel from Manzoni to Svevo* (Carbondale and Edwardsville, Southern Illinois University Press, 1967) pp. 149–83 (a short introduction and bibliography), and F.C. Bloodgood and J.W. Van Voorhis, 'Criticism of Italo Svevo: a Selected Checklist' in *Modern Fiction Studies*, vol. 18 (1972), i, pp. 119–29.

Useful brief introductions to Svevo in Italian, with bibliographies, are G. Spagnoletti, 'Italo Svevo', in *Letteratura italiana – I contemporanei* (Milan, Marzorati, 1963), vol. I, pp. 1–26, and G. Pampeloni, 'Italo Svevo', in *Storia della letteratura italiana*, direttori E. Cecchi, N. Sapegno, vol. IX, *Il Novecento* (Milan, Garzanti, 1969), pp. 493–532.

Additional references to items dealing with particular aspects of Svevo's work are given below.

CHAPTER ONE: Essays and Explorations
See especially:
G.P.BIASIN, 'Documenti per Svevo: dal diario di Elio Schmitz' in *Modern Language Notes* 83 (1968) 1, 107–25 (also in *Belfagor* 23 (1968) 1, 78–90
A.L.DE CASTRIS, 'Note Sveviane' in *Annali della Facoltà di Lettere e Filosofia dell'Università di Bari* 2 (1965) 215–65
B. MOLONEY, 'Svevo as a Jewish Writer' in *Italian Studies* XXVIII (1973)
E. SACCONE, 'Dati per una storia del primo Svevo (1880–1889)' in *La rassegna della letteratura italiana* 66 (1962) 3, 483–512
G. SPAGNOLETTI, 'La giovinezza e la formazione letteraria di Italo Svevo' in *Studi Urbinati* 27 (1953) 1–2, 179–221
For the intellectual background to Svevo's work see:
A. BOUISSY, 'Les fondements idéologiques de l'œuvre d'Italo Svevo' in *Revue des études italiennes* 12 (1966) 209–45, 350–73; 13 (1967) 23–50
A. ABRUZZESE, 'Da Trieste a Firenze. Lavoro e tradizione letteraria' in L. Strappini, C. Micocci, A. Abruzzese, *La classe dei colti. Intellettuali e società nel primo Novecento italiano* (Bari 1970) 205–311

CHAPTER TWO: Plays
A. AMATO, *La genesi narrativa di Italo Svevo* (Cosenza 1966)
A. MOMO, 'Il teatro di Italo Svevo' in *Ateneo Veneto* 5 (1967) 107–31
B. WEISS, 'Svevo's *Inferiorità*' in *Modern Fiction Studies* 18 (1972) 1, 33–44

CHAPTER THREE: First Narrative Fiction
A.L.DE CASTRIS, 'I racconti di Italo Svevo' in *Letteratura* 7 (1959) nos 37–8, 93–113, then in *Decadentismo e realismo – Note e discussioni* (Bari, n.d., but 1960)
P. ROBISON, '*Una vita* and the Family Romance' in *Modern Fiction Studies* 18 (1972) 1, 33–44
E. SACCONE, 'Il primo racconto di Italo Svevo' (on *L'assassinio ...*) in *Filologia e letteratura* 12 (1966) 93–112, 200–18
G. SAVARESE, 'Scoperta di Schopenhauer e crisi del naturalismo nel primo Svevo' in *La rassegna della letteratura italiana* 75 (1971) 3, 411–31
T.F. STALEY, 'The Growth of the Anti-hero: the Influence of *Le Rouge et le Noir* on Italo Svevo's *Una Vita*' in *Essays on Italo Svevo*, edited by T.F. Staley (Tulsa 1969) 3–13

CHAPTER FOUR: *Senilità*
S. BATTAGLIA, 'La coscienza della realtà nei romanzi di Svevo' in *Filologia e letteratura* 10 (1964) 225–48
J.A. GATT-RUTTER, '*Senilità* and the Unsaid' in *Essays on Italo Svevo*, ed. Staley, 14–34
R. PFOHL, 'Imagery as Disease in *Senilità*', in *Modern Language Notes* 76 (1964) 2, 143–50
E. SACCONE, '*Senilità* di Italo Svevo: dalla "impotenza del privato" alla "ansiosa speranza"' in *Modern Language Notes* 82 (1967) 1, 1–55

SELECT BIBLIOGRAPHY

CHAPTER FIVE: The Years of Silence
M. DAVID, *Letteratura e psicanalisi* (Milan 1967)
— *La psicoanalisi nella cultura italiana*, 2nd ed. (Turin 1970)
J. A. GATT-RUTTER, 'Non-commitment in Italo Svevo', *Journal of European Studies* 3 (1973) 2
S. JOYCE, *The Meeting of Svevo and Joyce* (Udine 1965)

CHAPTER SIX: *La coscienza di Zeno*
J. FRECCERO, 'Zeno's last cigarette' in *Modern Language Notes* 77 (1962) 1, 3–23, then in *From 'Verismo' to Experimentalism: Essays on the Modern Italian Novel*, edited by S. Pacifici (Bloomington and London 1969) 35–60
B. MOLONEY, 'Psychoanalysis and Irony in *La coscienza di Zeno*' in *Modern Language Review* 67 (1972) 2, 309–18
J. POUILLON, '*La Conscience de Zeno*: roman d'une psychanalyse' in *Les Temps Modernes* 10 (1954) 106 555–62
G. ROSOWSKI, 'Théorie et pratiques psychanalytiques dans la *Conscience de Zeno*' in *Revue des Études Italiennes* 16 (1970) 1, 49–70
E. SACCONE, 'Svevo, Zeno e la psicoanalisi' in *Modern Language Notes* 85 (1970) 1, 67–82

CHAPTER SEVEN: Last Narrative Fiction
E. BONORA, 'Inediti di Italo Svevo. Postilla a un ritratto critico' in *Gli ipocriti di Malebolge e altri studi di letteratura italiana e francese* (Milan and Naples 1953) 106–11
A. L. DE CASTRIS, 'I racconti di Italo Svevo' in *Decadentismo e realismo – Note e discussioni* (Bari, n.d., but 1960) 29–69
P. ROBISON, '*Una burla riuscita*: Irony as Hoax in Svevo' in *Modern Fiction Studies* 18 (1972) 1, 65–80
T. WLASSICS, 'Sulla *Novella* di Svevo' in *Nuova Antologia* 2046 (1971) 248–55

CHAPTER EIGHT: Autobiography and Art
C. BO, 'Per un ritratto di Svevo' in *Riflessioni critiche* (Florence 1953) 443–64
T. KEZICH, *Svevo e Zeno – Vite parallele* (Milan 1971)
G. LUTI, 'Il carattere di Ettore Schmitz' in *Narrativa italiana dell'Otto e Novecento* (Florence 1964) 109–66
N. TEDESCO, 'Autobiografia e invenzione in Italo Svevo' in *Filologia e Letteratura* 12 (1966) 430–54

CHAPTER NINE: Language, Style and Techniques
D. CERNECCA, 'Note sulla lingua di Italo Svevo' in *Studia Romanica et Anglica Zagabriensia* 9–10 (1960) 53–74, part of which has been republished as 'Dialectal Element and Linguistic Complex in Italo Svevo' translated by R. Treitel, in *Modern Fiction Studies* 18 (1972) 1, 81–9
— 'Le due redazioni di *Senilità* di Italo Svevo' in *Studia Romanica et Anglica Zagabriensia* 11 (1961) 29–66
G. DEVOTO, 'Decenni per Svevo' in *Studi di stilistica* (Florence 1950) 175–93

CHAPTER TEN: Italo-German Novelist
L. R. FURST, 'Italo Svevo's *La coscienza di Zeno* and Thomas Mann's *Der Zauberberg*' in *Contemporary Literature* 9 (1968) 492–506
D. C. MUECKE, *The Compass of Irony* (London 1969)
— *Irony* (London 1970, *The Critical Idiom* series, vol. 13)

INDEX

Abba, M., 26
Alberti, L.B., 10
Apollonio, A., 17, 18, 25
Ariosto, L., 17, 18

Barmant, C., 2
Bartolini, L., 46
Battaglia, S., 39, 41
Beach, J.W., 39
Bebel, F.A., 53
Bellow, S., 84, 125
Benco, S., 26, 56, 89, 113
Benelli, S., 19
Berto, G., 125
Boccaccio, G., 11
Booth, W.C., 103
Boswell, J., 68
Bragg, M., 125
Braine, J., 37
Brown-Sequard, C.E., 123
Bruni, G., 9
Buzzati, D., 125

Cappelli, L., 67
Capuana, L., 13, 27, 35
Carducci, G., 6, 10, 14, 18
Cernecca, D., 110, 111, 112, 113
Cesari, G., 3
Chamisso, A. von, 84
Cherbuliez, V., 9-10
Corriere della sera, 8, 96
Cossa, P., 19
Critica sociale, 52
Croce, B., 61, 108-9

D'Annunzio, G., 80
Dante Alighieri, 11
Darwin, C.R., 9, 11, 53, 62, 83, 105, 122
De Amicis, E., 8, 13, 27
De Castris, A.L., 34, 46
De Sanctis, F., 5, 9, 11
Devoto, G., 111
Diderot, D., 86
Dionisotti, C., 108
Domenica del Fracassa, 8
Domenica letteraria, 8
Dostoyevski, F., 29, 125

Ellmann R., 61
Enright, D.J., 43

Ferrari, P., 12, 17, 19
Finzi, A., 62
Finzi, I., 56
Flaubert, G., 14, 42, 46, 125
Fogazzaro, A., 8, 13
France, A., 9, 10, 116
Freud, S., 36, 60-3, 68, 69, 70, 71, 72, 73, 79, 101, 126
Fried, A., 64
Friedman, B.J., 84
Fucini, R., 110
Furbank, P.N., 32, 44, 60, 128
Furst, L.R., 127

Gatt-Rutter, J.G., 44, 49, 50
Giacosa, C., 12, 17
Giotti, V., 5
Goethe, J.W. von, 10, 17, 18, 79, 100, 126, 130
Gogol, N.V., 3
Goncourt, E. and J., 9, 121
Grita, S., 46

Hardy, T., 109
Hegel, G.W.F., 43, 86, 87
Heine, H., 7, 84, 127
Hemmings, F.J.W., 14
Heyse, P., 56
Hoffmann, E.T.A., 127

Ibsen, H.J., 19, 26, 59
Indipendente L', 5, 6-7, 15, 16, 20, 26-7, 28, 31, 39, 56

Jahier, V., 63
Jean-Paul (pseud.), *see* Richter
Jonard, N., 44, 58, 59, 99, 100
Joyce, J., 45, 60-1, 73, 98, 101, 125
Jung, C.G., 101

Kafka, F., 63, 125
Kezich, T., 17

Larbaud, V., 89
Leavis, F.R., 27
Lemaître, J., 9, 13

Index

Macerata, R., 2
Machiavelli, N., 9, 10, 104
Maier, B., 44, 111
Mailer, N., 2, 125
Mann, T., 61, 125, 126, 127, 128, 129, 130
Manzoni, A., 4, 14, 27, 61, 104, 108
Marin, B., 5
Marx, K. H., 9, 35, 52, 83, 85
Maupassant, G. De, 32
Maxia, S., 41, 49, 85, 127
Mayer, T., 1
Michelangelo, 10
Michelet, J., 9
Michelstaedter, C., 5
Momo, A., 21
Montale, E., 25, 39, 56, 113
Moravia, A., 48, 125
Morris, W., 53
Musil, R., 81, 85, 125, 126, 127, 129
Mussolini, B., 80

Napoleon Bonaparte, 9, 103
Nazione, La, 65
Nietzsche, F., 9, 79-80, 87, 101
Nuova Antologia, 8

Ohnet, G., 9, 10, 13
Oliva, D., 96
Olivier, L., 7

Pavese, C., 98
Petrarch, F., 37, 104, 126
Pfohl, R., 44
Piccolo, Il, 1, 8
Piccolo della sera, Il, 89
Pirandello, L., 23, 26, 110, 127-8
Proust, M., 91, 125

Renan, E., 9, 10-11
Richter, J.-P., 126, 127
Rietti, A., 58
Riffaterre, M., 114
Robbe-Grillet, A., 125
Rocca, E., 98
Rosenfeld, I., 84
Roth, H., 2
Roth, P., 2, 125

Saba, U., 5
Saccone, E., 11, 44, 99
St Thomas Aquinas, 61
Sardou, V., 12, 13
Sartre, J.-P., 79
Sassoon, S., 3
Scarfoglio, E., 9
Schiller, J. C. F., 10, 126
Schlegel, A., 126, 127
Schlegel, F., 126, 127
Schmitz, Adolfo (the elder), 2
Schmitz, Adolfo (the younger), 3, 4, 58
Schmitz, Aron *detto* Ettore, *see* Svevo
Schmitz, E., 3, 8, 26, 28, 99
Schmitz, F., 2, 3, 5, 102
Schmitz, Letizia, 102
Schmitz, Livia Veneziani, 2-3, 56, 57, 58
Scholom Aleichem, 84
Schopenhauer, A., 3, 9, 30, 34, 37, 61, 105, 106, 117, 126, 127
Schucking, W., 64
Shakespeare, W., 3, 7, 11, 13, 126, 127
Shaw, G. B. S., 26
Slataper, S., 4-5
Spagnoletti, G., 99
Spaini, A., 5
Spencer, H., 9, 19, 34, 35, 53, 83, 120, 129
Spenser, E., 130
Spriano, P., 55
Steinach, E., 123
Stendhal, 14, 32, 121, 125
Storey, D., 92, 125
Stuparich, G., 5
Svevo, I.
  education, 3, 5, 27
  irredentism, 1, 6-7, 64
  Jewishness, 1-3, 7-8, 61, 83-5, 101, 106, 128
  pacifism, 64
  pseudonyms, 1, 3-4, 7-8, 18, 28, 31
  'second self', 63, 103-4
  Socialism, 18, 64
  spiritualism, 21
Svevo, I. (Works)
  Essays: *La corruzione dell' anima*,

Svevo, I. (Works)—contd.
85, 87; *L'uomo e la teoria darwiniana*, 85; *Soggiorno londinese*, 63; *Sulla teoria della pace*, 64-6
Narrative fiction: *Cimutti*, 58-9, 111; *Corto viaggio sentimentale*, 90, 99, 105, 121, 123; *Giacomo*, 59; *Il malocchio*, 122; *Il mio ozio*, 25, 92, 93, 123; *Il vecchione*, 91, 92; *Incontro di vecchi amici*, 99; *In Serenella*, 58-9; *La buonissima madre*, 122; *La coscienza di Zeno, passim; La madre*, 89, 101; *La morte*, 95; *La novella del buon vecchio e della bella fanciulla*, 60, 95-6, 105, 110, 112; *L'assassinio di Via Belpoggio*, 7, 14, 28, 30, 99; *La tribú*, 35, 52-3; *L'avvenire dei ricordi*, 4; *Le confessioni del vegliardo*, 91, 92-4, 100; *Marianno*, 58-9, 111; *Orazio Cima*, 28, 59-60, 67, 122; *Proditoriamente*, 94-5; *Senilità, passim; Umbertino*, 25, 92-3; *Una burla riuscita*, 13, 99; *Una lotta*, 7, 28; *Una vita, passim; Un contratto*, 92, 93-4; *Vino generoso*, 60, 65-6, 67
Newspaper articles, 7-15, 28, 46, 65, 79, 128
Plays: *Ariosto governatore*, 16, 17-18; *Atto unico*, 16, 21, 22; *Con la penna d'oro*, 17, 24-5; *Il ladro in casa*, 16, 19-20; *Inferiorità*, 16, 17, 19, 23-4; *La rigenerazione*, 17, 25-6, 123; *La verità*, 17, 19, 23; *L'avventura di Maria*, 16, 20, 21, 58; *Le ire di Giuliano*, 17, 18, 19; *Le teorie del conte Alberto*, 17, 18-19; *Prima del ballo*, 16, 20; *Terzetto spezzato*, 16, 21, 22; *Una commedia inedita*, 17, 18, 19; *Un marito*, 16, 17, 21-3, 58
Miscellaneous: *Diario per la fidanzata*, 14, 69; *Epistolario*, 8, 60, 63, 84; *Profilo autobiografico*, 3, 5-6, 28, 60, 64, 111
Themes: 'Bovarysme', 23, 28, 30, 31, 36, 37-8, 40, 44, 45, 51-2, 55, 59, 77, 83, 99, 104, 105, 107, 118, 119,

Svevo, I., (Works)—contd.
127, 129; Darwinism, 11, 18-19, 33-4, 48, 52, 62, 85, 86, 87, 105, 120, 122, 126, 129; death, 25, 37, 93, 94-5, 112; determinism, 45, 77, 87, 100; egoism, 20, 30, 35, 47, 66, 67, 83, 94, 95, 128, 130; ethical alternative, 30, 35, 37, 41, 80, 106, 130; guilt, 44, 52, 60, 68, 73, 78, 79, 83, 92-3, 100, 106; health, 4, 42, 44, 47, 48, 55, 59, 61, 69, 75, 80, 83, 87, 91, 93, 130; illness, 47, 50, 55, 61, 68-9, 73, 75, 79, 80, 87, 93, 99; marriage, 19, 20, 21, 23, 122; memory, 25, 52, 91; money, 24, 25, 48, 53, 66, 93, 94, 95, 96, 122; music, 6, 7, 9, 58, 76, 77, 99, 120-2; old age, 4, 25, 81, 92, 94, 123; rejuvenation, 25, 93, 123; renunciation, 34, 37, 57-8, 77; science, 9, 35, 36, 93, 128; smoking, 4, 9, 68, 71, 73, 93, 99, 101-2; Socialism, 18, 35, 48, 52-5, 65-6, 92, 94, 99-100, 129; society, 26, 29, 30, 33-5, 38, 41, 45, 52-3, 82, 86-7, 105, 106, 128-9, 130; superman, 31, 79-80, 87, 104; surprise, 30, 49, 119, 120; time, 41, 42, 43, 49, 72, 91, 94; truth, 10-11, 13, 70, 75-6, 83; visual arts, 9, 59, 120-1; war, 26, 63-4, 81-3, 92, 95, 100, 106, 128; work, 34, 57, 59, 77, 79, 82-3, 92, 99

Taine, H. A., 9, 11, 79
Thiers, L. A., 9
Tolstoy, L., 79, 125
Torelli, A., 12
Trilling, L., 86
Turati, F., 52

Veneziani, B., 61
Veneziani, O., 21, 57, 59
Verga, G., 10, 13, 14, 27, 39, 108
Veruda, U., 46, 102, 121
Vettori, F., 104
Voronoff, S., 123

Wagner, R., 9, 98

Weiss, E., 61, 63
Wisse, R.R., 84

Yeats, W.B., 123

Zergol, G., 105
Zola, E., 9, 10, 11, 14, 35, 121, 125
Zweig, A., 101